THE PHILOSOPHY OF SELF-KNOWLEDGE

About the Author

M.M. Agrawal has done his graduation and doctorate in philosophy from University of London. He has subsequently taught at the following institutions:

Northern Polytechnic, London; University of Khartoum, Sudan; University of Nigeria, Nigeria; North-Eastern Hill University, Shillong, where he held the chair of culture.

He was also a fellow at the Indian Institute of Advanced Study, Shimla.

Among his numerous publications on various subjects, his following works in the Philosophy of Religion and Spirituality are considered as noteable contribution to knowledge; *Individuality and Reincarnation* (1978), *The Philosophy of Non-Attachment* (1982), *Consciousness and the Integrated Being* (1991), *Ethics and Spirituality* (1998), *Freedom of the Soul* (2002), *Spirituality and Indian Culture* (2005).

THE PHILOSOPHY OF SELF-KNOWLEDGE

M.M. AGRAWAL

CONCEPT PUBLISHING COMPANY PVT. LTD.,
NEW DELHI-110059

ISBN-13: 978-81-8069-708-1

First Published 2010

Published and Printed by

Concept
Since 1974

Concept Publishing Company Pvt. Ltd.
Regd. Office:
A/15-16, Commercial Block, Mohan Garden
New Delhi-110059 (India)
Phones : 25351460, 25351794, *Fax* : 091-11-25357109
Email : publishing@conceptpub.com,
Website: www.conceptpub.com

Editorial Office:
H-13, Bali Nagar, New Delhi-110 015, India.

Cataloging in Publication Data--*Courtesy:* D.K. Agencies (P) Ltd. <docinfo@dkagencies.com>

Agrawal, M. M. (Murari Mohan), 1937-
The philosophy of self-knowledge / M.M. Agrawal.
p. cm.
Includes index.
ISBN 9788180697081

1. Self-knowledge, Theory of. 2. Knowledge, Theory of (Hinduism) I. Title.

DDC 121 22

Preface

The quest of a complete experiential knowledge of the self is absolutely central to Indian spirituality. And, it is rightly thought that without knowing the nature and the destiny of the self, we can form no idea of any fundamental goals and purposes in life, since the latter exist only for the self in the first place. We can only move around willy-milly in the world pursuing the goals thrown up by the environment in one's present social milieu, but without any ultimate meaning or significance or intrinsic goodness. Self-knowledge, thus, imparts direction and rationale to an otherwise chaotic pursuit of the desire to be, in a largely chaotic social world. All the same, this book is written with the insight, that self-knowledge should not be placed in some esoteric realm of meditation and mysticism. It must begin with the day-to-day understanding of human existence in relationship. The individual must come to realize that both in his mind and in his body, he is constituted of the material in his natural and social environment. The entire conceptual repertoire of the mind and the biological material of his body do not come under "private property". The individual is constantly nourished, both in his mind and body, by the "outside". And in this sense he is inseparable from the whole. In the ultimate analysis, his individuality is no more than that of a 'wave in the ocean'.

And this realization comes with the force of enlightenment. It brings freedom from the self-centered existence set by the conditioned mind, and puts the individual in the world of eternal creativity.

In another way, we can see the necessity and priority of self-knowledge over other forms of objective knowledge. When we look at the human condition as reflected in the constitution of our own selves, we find a state of utter confusion. Human mind is saddled with great fear and anxiety and torn by perpetual conflict. The desire to 'become' is a symptom of this conflict. What is the cause of this state of mind of the human being? Knowing the cause and knowing the way of ending it is self-knowledge. The cause is within the individual and any same person must work to banish it from his psyche.

M.M. Agrawal

Acknowledgement

I am grateful to Prof. S.C. Malik for making his personal library at Mukteshwar, available to me for study.

M.M. Agrawal

Contents

1

Introduction

Man has always sought something 'more' and 'better' than what he has at the moment. In face of a hostile nature and woes of survival, he is constantly seeking security, comfort, pleasure and power, both quantitatively and qualitatively. To that end he has built civilisations, pursued sciences and the arts. With his intelligence, technological skills and knowledge he has transformed his surroundings and considerably improved the so-called 'quality of his life'. But, individually, he seems to have remained self-centred, self-seeking and morally irresponsible for the 'whole' to which he inalienably belongs.

This is so, perhaps, because he sees that as an individual human being, his life is short and sorrowful, always remaining somewhat unfulfilled, and struggling and constantly threatened by conflicts, ailments, old age and death. He can never win over the hazards of the 'human condition' to which he is condemned. So he turns to religion to find God and heaven and a life of endless pleasures beyond this world of time and death. But unfortunately, in this religious turn too, the logic of his worldly pursuits remains the same. He is still seeking 'something more and better' for his individual self.

In India, however, and amongst ancient civilisations, perhaps only in India, something completely different happened. Apart from the usual religious turn, the people turned to themselves to seek out the truth about the "seeker" himself. It seemed obvious to their logical minds that without knowing their own nature and their own status, in the scheme of reality as a whole, searching for 'more and better' in this life or in life after, is sheer madness. For, it may be that he has all the wealth of eternal happiness hidden within his own soul which he himself hid away and forgotten! May be he needs nothing from the world outside of him except, of course, what is necessary for a human life? He has only to discover the treasure within and realise that all the seeking is unnecessary and based in the ignorance of the true nature of the self. And again, quite obviously, to know the true nature of the self they have to look within themselves. In this journey each one is alone and nothing from outside can give one self-knowledge. Their quest, therefore, remained essentially secular, though it often overlapped the path of religion. Their central question in this enquiry was: 'Who or what am I?'

For thousands of years now, many individuals have undertaken this enquiry and found the truth. And each of them has found that their enquiry into the nature of the individual self refers them to find out the truth about reality as a whole. This is so because to know any individual "completely" one has to know how it will respond in all possible situations in all possible worlds; and so to know the self one will have to know how one's self is placed vis-a-vis the reality as a whole. Since, literally speaking, one cannot watch oneself in "all possible situations"; one has to understand how one is related to the primordial forces constituting the human condition. And then, further, one will have to understand what would be the state of the self when it breaks away from the human condition into the realm of the transcendental. In this way, the highest point of self-knowledge is well expressed in the Advaita philosophy of Shankara in the well-known dictum: "*jivo brahmaiva na parah*", that is "the self is not distinct from Brahman", where the latter is conceived as 'one all inclusive reality'.

The technological advancements have not solved any human problems. Wars have continued throughout the 20th century. The computer revolution have alienated man from man. The systemic violence and corruption have brought about a collapse of values and consequently a collapse of its own economy. All these are symptoms of a deeper problem which is, that man has sought 'more and better' only in the outer world, with a total neglect of the inner psychological world. It is in the latter that all human problems arise and solving them would naturally require self-knowledge.

Self

It is generally recognised that the peculiarity of the self consists in the fact that it is perennially a subject, the 'knower', and can never be turned into an object, the 'known'. But that is not all. More importantly, the peculiarity is not simply that it is the knower, but also that in all its acts of knowing, simultaneously, it also knows itself to be the knower of knowledge. This fact can be appreciated only from the 'inside'. The self is constantly, by its integrating power of self-awareness, putting all its perceptions into a single mind. That is, from the inside, the self knows that all these perceptions "belong" to him. There is a sense of "mineness" about them. It "owns" them in a special way, not from the "outside", as it owns a house, for example, but in a way which signifies that the perceptions in question "mingle" with its own being.

What has just been said is true of all other elements in the mind of the self — the sensations, desires, thoughts, will, etc. Yet the self can't be identified with the mind. This is so because in knowing that the mind belongs to it, it turns the mind into an 'object' of introspection and puts it psychologically at a distance from itself. It 'objectifies' the mind and itself remains the perennial subject. All along it knows its subject-status non-cognitively i.e. intuitively. Next, it also knows from the inside that the events and states of the mind come and go, while its self-awareness remains constantly focused on one and the same entity, the self, which undergoes many different states but sticks to none, it does not identify itself with any one of them exclusively. This leads to the third reason why the self can't be identified with the mind. The self is a simple entity while the mind is a complex one. The mind is an 'ensemble' of many qualitatively different states having a psychological structure in time. But the self has only one quality (if it can be called that) of consciousness, which is pure and simple in the sense that no descriptive concepts can be applied to it. Of course one can describe a particular state of consciousness in terms of the object it is aware of. But that won't be a description of the intrinsic quality of consciousness, especially considered as a subject or the knower.

The mind, which is also called the "empirical self", is given that name simply because it is accessible to empirical investigation in "introspection". But the entity to which the empirical self is available for introspective knowledge is itself not so available. It remains the subject and, therefore, the true self which can't be identified with the mind or the empirical self. Introspection is always 'after the event', since the object of knowledge must already exist before it is known.

So, it turns out that self is accessible to one in two ways. First, as mentioned earlier, it is accessible in a direct intuition of itself as the 'knower of knowledge' and then in a secondary sense, in introspection, it is available as the primary acts of cognition of the external world. The self can be absorbed in its cognitions at the 'primary' level, as indeed it normally is in day-to-day living, without simultaneously, but non cognitively, being aware of itself in those modes of cognition. And then later it may, introspectively, become aware that it had such and such cognitions. The introspective knowledge of its own primary cognitive activity, however, will be a second hand knowledge because it is based in memory and therefore conceptual. Such knowledge belongs to the mind. So, for true self-knowledge, as it will be clear shortly, it is the simultaneous, non-cognitive awareness of itself that is more significant. The simultaneous self-awareness is direct, non-conceptual and ever-new with the emerging flow of consciousness. Since this nature of the self can be grasped only from the 'inside', self-knowledge is never merely conceptual; it is more of a personal and experiential nature.

For similar reasons, the self can't be identified with the body either. First, the sense of 'being the body' is derivative. It is given through the experience of kinaesthetic sensations which suggest that the self is occupying a body, in the psychological space. Later, we learn to identify the psychological space with the physical body which we call 'mine'. Next, the body is a complex entity known cognitively but the self, as we have seen, must be a simple entity (doing a complex job of organising sensations) known in direct non-cognitive awareness. And what is known about the self in this way is simply negative – that it is not any of the things that it knows cognitively. So, the empirical self hides the essential nature of the self which consists simply of "being-consciousness". This core identity of the self does not signify a cognitive awareness of itself. As we have seen, it is a non-cognitive accompaniment to all its cognitive states in which the self becomes aware of the external world. This essential nature of the self as pure being consciousness is to be discovered by putting aside both its bodily and mental identities. The great tradition of yogic meditation teaches how to make this discovery and remain steadfastly established in one's essential self. The experience of reality in this state is rightly said to be indescribable. Naturally, when the mind, which is a network of concepts, has been put aside, knowledge in the ordinary sense of the word is not available. Then knowing will be a kind of "being", which is the essential nature of the self.

The empirical self, with which we identify ourselves, as we will see shortly, arises in the response of thought to reality, and in that sense, carries a sense of temporality about itself. It sees itself as short-lived and fears its extinction. Only complete self-knowledge can reveal this truth and make free the individual from the primordial fear of life.

In our basic conception of the self, the sense of being a body plays a crucial role. But we also ascribe to the self a number of non-bodily achievements such as the higher skills involved in creative activities and scientific pursuit and social manipulations. These higher level engagements have, in a complicated way, to do with memories and non-computable events and qualities such as 'insights', 'inspirations', emotions, love and moral intuitions. So, taken together, all of these make up what we call our 'self' in everyday talk, and to which we attribute 'individuality' and substantiality.

But, honestly speaking, our self-awareness does not refer us to a single simple entity, a mental substance, which manages all the factors noted above – the sense of being a body and higher skills etc. – and yet retains, its separate identity. True, I have the consciousness that I am a separate distinct entity, but in reality, there is no one entity to correspond to this consciousness. And, from the fact that my consciousness tells me that I am a separate individual self, over and above having a sense of being a body and a mind, it does not follow that I am really such a self.

The truth is that all the attributes comprising my 'self' seem to be drawn from two "sources of all energy" – the material source and consciousness. Let 'breath' represent the source of material energy and "consciousness" represent the other forms of energy which we have mentioned. Then the picture that emerges of ourselves clearly suggests that we cannot be or exist as we do, without constantly drawing from both these types of the sources of energy. Take the sense of being a body. It is obviously constituted by the kinaesthetic sensations that arise within the body which itself is kept alive by constant breathing. Now the important point that I want to make is that the breath is not "my" in any important sense of the term. Initially, it has to come from "all breath". And I recognise it as my breath only after it has serviced my body and is going out. I cannot call it "my" when it is coming in. So the body is not a separate substantial individual in any absolute sense.

Similar considerations apply to my sense of being an individual mind. When consciousness manifests as a thought in me initially it comes from the source of "all consciousness". And only when I have made sense of it and I am expressing it in behaviour or language, that I am entitled to call it "my" thought. In other words, for our mental life, we are all drawing from a common source of energy which is called "consciousness". So again the conclusion reached is that, even as individual minds, we are not radically and substantially separate from each other and from the universal source of "all energy", assuming that at the level of energy both forms of energy cannot be separated as emanating from independent identifiable sources. And further, the more important truth it suggests is that all living beings are "interconnected" and "interdependent" in sharing resources from the same common impersonal source of all energy. Literally, as ancient sages realised, "all mankind belongs to one family". This makes each of us responsible for the "whole" to which we inalienably belong.

This piece of self-knowledge abolishes the myth of radically separate individualities. But it also exhorts us to seek out the truth about the nature of that "whole" itself, to which we integrally belong. The quest of self-knowledge, therefore, refers one to the quest of truth or the ultimate nature of being as a whole.

Thus, self-knowledge at the very basic level, consisting of "being an inalienable part of an interconnected and interdependent whole", therefore, prompts us to seek out the nature of the very essence of being, or the ground reality of all beings. Self-knowledge therefore is not simply either the knowledge of individual biographies of 'who am I?' as a so and so, or even added to it, the knowledge of the workings of the individual minds in terms of their operational desires, motives and beliefs etc., though these forms of knowledge about oneself must be included in a complete picture of the self.

The complete picture will include other higher forms of self-knowledge in the following order. First, as we have noted above, there is the knowledge of 'who I am' as a social unit. This will include information about my bodily identity as well as to the social groups to which I belong. It will include knowledge of my physical abilities and how I perform in social situations. Above this and higher than this will be the knowledge of my empirically accessible mind – mental skills, likes and dislikes, intellectual and artistic abilities, aspirations and ambitions, etc. Next, and in spiritual taxonomy, higher than this, will be the deeper knowledge of my hidden self – the unconscious, which regulates my emotional choices, my depressions and ecstasies, my neurotic or heroic behaviours etc. Often we need psychiatric or meditational help to bring this part of the self to light.

But there are still, spiritually most significant, forms of self-knowledge. The first of these is the knowledge of the 'primordial forces' of life providing the very structure of the human condition within which each individual personal-self is constituted. The three that I have selected for discussion in the following chapters are embedded in the nature of consciousness. The knowledge and understanding of their operations is most important for total self-knowledge and consequently for enlightenment. These are: primordial fear, psychological becoming and attachment.

Of these, the first is the fear of non-being or self-annihilation. It arises due to the fact that in a conceptual apprehension, consciousness, which is fundamental to being, appears to be perpetually disturbed – it dies as it rises. And this gives rise to great insecurity about the existence of the self which is perceived to have a continuity throughout one's life. The fear which this feature of consciousness generates, assumes a myriad of forms in day-to-day life. It is most commonly apprehended in the form of 'the fear of losing one's memory' or losing the things and people to whom you are deeply attached. And, of course, the most suppressed fear: the fear of sudden death. Next, becoming is the psychological process of assuming new identities, such as, becoming a wealthy man, famous and powerful – all these in the psychological dimension. Continuous gathering of riches, etc. and continuous search for fulfilment, are manifestations of the need to 'become'. Becoming also gives the false sense of continuity of one and the same self-identity. The human reality, which Sartre has described as "the desire to be", is made actual through constant becoming. In everyday life, "the desire to be" translates into constant thinking which is a mild form of experiencing and, of course, the desire to go on "experiencing" which signifies continuous becoming.

And thirdly, the primordial force of "attachment" is most significant in the context of the quest of the knowledge of the self. Attachment is generated naturally to all those things, people and ideas which provide pleasure, hope and a sense of personal security. The relative strength of each attachment would depend upon the degree of security etc. they are believed to provide. Since attachments are stored up in memories, the passage of time will naturally weaken them appropriately.

We can see from these general considerations that some attachments must run very deep in our lives and regulate our conduct often through complex and unconscious motives. Understanding the structure and the modus operandi of attachments, therefore, must be a very important part of our quest of the knowledge of the self.

Indeed freedom from the whole structure of attachments has been the central concern of spirituality in all the religions of Indian origin. It almost defines the character of the mind of an enlightened saint or a "jivanmukti" i.e. a person who has attained freedom from sorrow in his present life and freedom from rebirth hereafter. And knowledge of the self is what opens up the door to the attainment of this blessed state of "non-attachment".

The way in which the complete knowledge of the self, therefore, will lead one to the highest spiritual abode – of infinite peace and eternal bliss – has to be appreciated at this point, so that we can see that the stipulated knowledge is neither simply an intellectual exercise nor simply a means of acquiring some occult powers to attain glory in worldly existence. The way it works is as follows:

We have seen that all the primordial forces constituting the self, which we have mentioned above, arise from a certain perception of the nature of consciousness. They all build upon the fact that consciousness is perceived as something "perpetually disturbed", "having no continuity" and feeling "insecure" at the thought of having no substantiality. But how is the consciousness 'perceived' at all? It has to be admitted that there is no direct perception of consciousness – a consciousness of consciousness, as it were – simply because it cannot be objectified. Our so-called "consciousness of consciousness" is non-cognitive. It arises simultaneously to an objective perception where an object is directly perceived, and it is delivered negatively as "I am not that thing of which I am conscious". This consciousness of consciousness does not give us any positive, or descriptive knowledge of the self. It only tells us that the self which perceives the objective entity is identical to the knowing consciousness. The knowing consciousness is always the 'subject' and never an 'object' and it possesses an "inner realisation" of the fact that it is the knower. Simply put, in perception one knows something objectively and knows subjectively that one knows.

But now the important question that arises is that if consciousness does not perceive itself 'directly', then how does it know that it is ephemeral and of which it is then fearful, insecure and seeking to become. Surely, the knowledge of these characteristics of consciousness must be conceptual arising in a response of thought to the reality of consciousness. The position seems like this.

Consciousness seems to exist as pure awareness, unowned by a separate entity which "possesses" consciousness, and it has the power of thought, by which it objectifies itself. It puts itself at a distance and sees itself as an individual ego. The individual ego is perceived in a limited way as the subject of that particular object which it perceives in the world. In a subsequent perception why it sees itself as the 'same' subject as the previous one is a phenomenon to be explained later. For the time being, I am only suggesting that it is the conceptual consciousness of consciousness that generates fear of non-being, because, not knowing consciousness in its essence, it interprets it as perpetually disturbed, placed in time and insecure.

So far then, consciousness knows itself only in the focus of its manifestation in thought. It does not give us complete knowledge of its nature in its essence. That is, self-knowledge which reveals and understands its primordial forces and their engagement with the world, does not reveal its transcendental nature, or its nature as 'being consciousness'. It does not tell us what is going on at the very "source" which creates thought in the first place. We have no idea of that power of the self which creates thought, and then knows itself through that thought as a temporal being – a subject of shifting states of consciousness.

Moreover, in this episode of creating thought and knowing itself through thought, it creates an illusion of knowledge that the empirical reality is the ultimate reality. However, in this whole creative exercise, consciousness has betrayed itself. It has, as we have seen, leaked out that consciousness of consciousness can be attained only in a non-cognitive awareness of itself as something which is not what it is objectively aware of. This point is important in the following way:

Firstly, it tells us that there is still a higher plane of self-knowledge. To indicate that it is the highest and ultimate form of knowledge, the world 'self' is written with a capital 's'. And secondly, that whenever and howsoever the higher self becomes known, it will have to accomplish an extraordinary feat of self-transcendence, that is, transcendence of the empirical self or the individual ego. This is because the non-cognitive mode of self-awareness cannot be called "knowledge" in the ordinary sense of the word. The self is perennially the 'subject' of knowledge, never the 'object' of knowledge. That is why, in the spiritual literature, for the knowledge of the highest self, the word "realisation" is used. At the highest level one realises that the true nature of the self is thus and so.

The Possibility of Complete Self-knowledge

We have seen above that the quest for self-knowledge is carried out in four different stages. First, there is the ordinary empirical knowledge of the self. Here one notices that the self passes through the familiar cognitive, conative and volitional states of mind. The self identifies itself with these states and knows them to be his own states. It also notices a connection within its states of consciousness. These states occur in a temporal sequential formation. And only through 'memory' one can hold on to them. Such knowledge is obtained through familiar acts of introspection.

And next, at a higher level, we acquire knowledge of the hidden, unconscious forces of the mind, which propel our mental states at the conscious level. These comprise both, our inherited biological instincts and propensities, as well as acquired tendencies, motives, intentions and desires etc. which are picked up from the environment we grow up in, and which are relegated to the unconscious. A large part of our lives is lived by the impulses we receive from the unconscious. It is ironical that though we are blindly moved by the hidden forces, the actions which we perform due to them at the conscious level, are identified by us as our "free choices". Self-knowledge removes this illusion and shows that the empirical self is more of a mechanical product of environment than a product of human essence.

This mechanical self is not the real 'doer', it is simply the 'translator' of the inner states into appropriate movements in the outer. Self-knowledge restores our true humanity in spiritual freedom and creativity. This higher form of self-knowledge is also obtained in introspection but of a subtler form. Because there is a continuum from the unconscious to the conscious, the hidden persuader of motives and desires, etc. can be caught by a very attentive mind at the very inception of a conscious act. If we are quietly alert and watchful of our behaviours, we can catch the culprit red-handed, as it were impelling us to act in a certain way. Here we encounter our hidden unconscious in its true colour. If we can stay put undisturbed with this encounter we will find that the compelling desires etc. loose their grip on our conscious life with respect to particular emotions which they are pushing forward. In case of obsessional forces, the encounter can result in a catharsis and normalise behaviour in the person experiencing it.

Now, in the still higher stage of self-knowledge, the knowledge of the primordial forces is categorical. The primordial forces which we have mentioned hide in every fold of conscious life. Indeed the mould of the human condition is prepared by these forces. To discover this fundamental mould of life and to know about these forces, therefore, we have to delve much deeper into ourselves and reach out to the very root of human behaviour. We have seen that the primordial forces take shape due to a certain perception of consciousness by thought. Thought sees consciousness as ephemeral, falling as it rises. Dying in the moment immediately after its birth seems to be the natural destiny of consciousness. Naturally, then conscious beings are afraid of this destiny and play all kinds of 'games' to hide this fact from themselves. They imagine an immortal self-separate and unique for each person which is indestructible. And life is lived accordingly under such beliefs in 'becoming' and 'attachment' along with fear. Again, it is a question of discovering if this perception of the nature of consciousness is correct. To make this discovery, therefore, one has to reach to the very moment of the inception of thought, and naturally of course, discover if consciousness can know itself without recourse to thought. That is, having reached to the point of its inception, thought has to abandon itself and one is left only with the consciousness of consciousness. Can this work? Fortunately, as we have said above, consciousness has, by its very nature, a non-cognitive aspect to it. As we have said, consciousness is always aware, in every cognition, that "it is not that thing of which it is conscious". Now, here, the "thing' in question is thought itself and consciousness is aware of having dropped it. It follows thus, that consciousness, in the act of ending thought, is non-cognitively aware that it is not the thought which it created and which it has dropped now.

We have entered now the fourth stage of self-knowledge. Here consciousness knows now that it has the power to create thought but it is not identical with it. In its absolute essence it is pure creativity. Simultaneously, one has also discovered the truth one was looking for at the third stage, namely, 'if the perception of thought with respect to the essential nature of consciousness were correct'. Thought perceived consciousness as having momentary existence. But now one sees that was a mistaken notion. Consciousness, though creates the world of thought, it is not identical with it. Instead consciousness in its essence is a timeless source of all creativity – "a source of all energy". So the third and fourth stages of self-knowledge are arrived at in one go. As soon as one reaches the point of inception of thought and leaves it behind, the truth reveals itself. The self-deception of consciousness by its own creative power of thought exists only at the empirical level. As soon as that has folded up the individual self has disappeared in the infinite and eternal ocean of consciousness. Surely this revelation must be an act of spiritual intuition. The introspective meditations must stop at the point of reaching the inception of thought.

To make both these stages of self-knowledge real in one's life, surely, one will have to make a serious effort in understanding life as a whole.

One will have to look at the broader picture and apprehend the overall character of life as it unfolds itself in its journey from birth to death. The various meditations in the Indian spiritual tradition aim at arriving at the point of inception of thought. One who arrives at this point perceives the act of creation of the thought-world. But this does not complete his quest for complete knowledge of the self. He has still to make the intuitive ascent into the transcendental "source of all energy" – a quantum jump, as it were, at the border of thought and the realm of pure consciousness, from thought into the world of absolute creation.

There does not seem to be a definite method or meditation prescribed for attaining this final feat of ascent. Not surprising, since all methods and meditations are conceptual and therefore cannot carry one beyond concept. At this point religion recommends a way out of the dilemma. It is the way of "surrender" to God and by His "grace" one will make the intuitive ascent in question. This much is said by the Lord Himself. In the Gita, Krishna says to Arjuna: "God is seated in the heart of all beings .... go to His refuge, surrender to Him in all your sentiments, and by His grace, you will receive the supreme peace and the abode of the eternal" (ch 18, 61-62). But the trouble with this recommendation is that "surrender" is not something which one can "make". It is not an act of individual will. It is something which has to "happen" to one – a state one has to walk into unknowingly, a state of complete devotion or "bhakti".

Again Krishna tells us of the conditions to be fulfilled which will lead one to embrace "bhakti" and to accomplish this final act of surrender. He tells us that "those who are aware of God's presence in the world, keeping cheerful, unlamenting and undemanding, living with total impartiality to all, they all receive my true 'bhakti'" (Gitā , ch 18, 54). So, on the psychological plane there is a whole orientation of life, a way of relating to others in impartiality, keeping one's grief, self-pity and ambitions aside, which one has to embrace before he can receive the gift of 'bhakti' or 'surrender in all one's sentiments'. Unfortunately, in the present day scenario, this inwardness of 'bhakti' is completely lost. It is reduced to a performance for "entertainment" in a religious context. For example, the practice of listening to the stories of Rama and Krishna, performing rituals of worship in the temple, dancing and singing (often in vulgar cinema tunes) for a popular musical experience, are far from fulfilling the conditions which Krishna lays down for receiving the gift of 'bhakti'.

So what is important for attaining the "final feat of ascent". is having those inner psychological states (cheerfulness, unlamenting, undemanding) and those ethical attitudes of impartiality and equal-mindedness in living one's daily life. And then, quite spontaneously, without asking for it, one may land into the domain beyond thought, where the ultimate true nature of the self is intuitively or non-cognitively revealed to him.

This point is made very clearly in the non-theistic strand of the Indian spirituality, which advocates total self-reliance in attaining the highest form of self-knowledge. They suggest, rightly in my view, that if the final step' can't be taken by the act of will then it is futile to try for it and to worry about not being able to do it and to search for alternative methods. One should rather do what one can do, namely, work on himself and transform himself inwardly, to realise those states and ethical attitudes of desirelessness and impartiality which we have mentioned above. In effect, the crucial elements in the required self-transformation are not different in the two traditions.

However, to attain the received self-transformation one will have to begin with the knowledge of the 'daily-self' or the familiar self. This self has an identity which is socially created. We can call it the "social-self". It exists only in relationship with the outside world. If you are asked to describe yourself or identify yourself, you will say things like: I am a father, I have a wife and three children, I have a house on the hills because I love nature, I am a professor of mathematics and so on. Your identity is a weave of relationships with people, things and ideas which are important to you. So to discover oneself, to have knowledge of the social self, one will have to be aware of the whole web of relationships that surrounds one and constitutes one. And this awareness will have to be not a casual one but with a serious intent of discovering the true nature of one's relationships. By "discovering the true nature" is meant discovering the motives and attitudes which are active in the background and which determine one's reactions and responses in the web of life.

In the 20th century, the most influential teacher of this awareness method' (if one may call it) has been J. Krishnamurti. He rightly maintains that since the self is manifest in all our behaviour, to know the self we have to watch ourselves, constantly in all our relationships. To get to the motives behind our actions we have to watch our thoughts, our attitudes, our speech in daily life in everyday relationship.

But the novelty of his approach lies in his suggestion of the "manner" in which we are to watch ourselves. Ordinarily, when we become aware of ourselves, we are simultaneously running a commentary on ourselves. That is, we are simultaneously evaluating our behaviour – we are condemning it or applauding it or correcting it. In this process we are distorting the truth. Whereas, if we 'simply observe', "just see the fact without judgment, without condemnation or acceptance", then there is the action of self-knowledge. His word for this way of observing is "choiceless awareness". The truth about oneself unfolds itself quite effortlessly in choiceless awareness. Of course, Krishnamurti realises that it is simpler said than done. Normally we would think that keeping oneself established in that kind of self-awareness itself would be quite effortful. But Krishnamurti gives the impression that it would not be so if one were really seriously interested in self-knowing. But this 'real serious interest' itself will have to be without any motive of self-advancement. And how is this motiveless state to come by? The only answer in Krishnamurti is that one has to open one's eyes to the realities of life: that one lives in fear, that one lives in attachment, that one lives in conflict constantly seeking to become. And all this ends in sorrow and eventually in death. But such perception has to be accompanied with the understanding that our so-called 'normal' but meaningless way of life is chosen because of the lack of self-knowledge. So there is a way out of the circularity. It is to "open one's eyes" and see why we live the way we live. For Krishnamurti this "seeing" why we live the 'self-seeking way' we live comes naturally when we have opened our eyes. And there can't be a method telling us how to open our eyes. Krishnamurti's faith in human capacity is immense. Just look around in choiceless awareness and the rest will follow.

Now, the important point that emerges from the reflections

above is that certain mental states and the ethical attitudes that are required in the theistic approach are the same in the non-theistic approach too. Basically, one has to put aside the ambitious self-seeking way of life and surrendering to "what is", God or Reality, in unlamenting and undemanding frame of mind, in total impartiality, receive the wisdom of self-knowledge.

Eventually the knowledge of the highest self has to be an effortless, spontaneous act of ascent in non-cognitive self-awareness, into the domain beyond thought. But one has to make oneself deserving of that act to happen. Both the theistic and the non-theistic approaches seem to me valid in this regard. The important thing is to do one's own bit and rise above the self-seeking motives. Then, remaining established in motiveless, self-awareness, allow the self-knowing truth to do its own bit. Of course, one wants that spontaneous act of ascent to happen to one. But this 'wanting' is motiveless in the sense that one doesn't want it as a "means" to achieving the highest spiritual status of possessing complete self-knowledge. It is not a movement of 'becoming'. One wants the highest knowledge of the self for the sake of it, that is, self-knowledge is possible only when the self is observed without the motive of enriching the self in any way – even morally and spiritually.

2

Of Bondage and Freedom

In the Indian rendition of life, the human condition is seen as that of "bondage" to the world. This bondage is perceptible only to very sensitive minds, in their contemplation and meditation; intellectual perception of the bondage is the first step towards "freedom" from it. Self-knowledge is the doorway to enlightenment which results in an unconditional freedom or *moksha* from the bondage to the world or *sansara*. Freedom is thus the natural goal of human life and the highest attainment of its spiritual endeavours. In the Indian spiritual tradition, this freedom can be attained either with or without the assistance of a personal God. In the Hindu religion, the philosophies of Sankhya and Yoga primarily invoke the latter. Similarly, Jain and Buddhist religions do not believe in the necessity of a supreme being or God or Ishwara, either to exist or to assist in the attainment of *moksha*. But other strands of Hinduism and the nascent Sikh religion do invoke Ishwara or a supreme being. But the state of *moksha* or the ultimate spiritual freedom is universally recognised as the highest spiritual goal of human life.

So, naturally understanding the nature of bondage and the fundamental characteristics of freedom is of paramount importance for any serious adventure with spirituality.

As we have said, bondage is not an obvious fact of nature. But the sensitive mind soon sees its intimations first in situations where he is 'compelled to do' such and such and 'compelled to be' in such and such postures in daily life. Then more deeply, if we look at life as a whole – a movement from birth to death – we can't fail to notice that in general a human being is constrained like an arrow in flight, first by his biology to be a certain kind of creature and then constrained by his psychology to live his conscious life driven by unconscious passions and attitudes into which he is conditioned in his upbringing. Both physically and mentally one has inherited a state of 'conditional being'. By the time he becomes aware of his separate identity, as an entity who can intend and choose and will independently of others he is already a 'made', a conditioned human being. By a certain age in the very childhood, he is complete, like a seed, to grow weakly or strongly in the future environment. But the grown-up adult sees himself as a "self" – a psychological centre endowed with a separate will. He sees himself as an agency of change in his own existential condition. He sees himself as the original source of thoughts and actions which he gives rise to *ab initio*, as it were, out of nothing, simply by his inherent power. He is, therefore, not identical with those thoughts and actions. Rather he is the sole independent original author of them. He thinks that all that happens to him happens through his own will and he is identical with this will.

But soon the truth begins to emerge. His belief about himself does not tally with his personal reality. And he is unable to locate himself as a transcendent self, over and above his experiences of life.

As we said earlier, the self is enmeshed in experiences. It is dragged into situations and compelled to identify itself with the thoughts and actions which proceed from him. This is not a situation of freedom of the will. He cannot account for all that happens to him in terms of his free will. In fact, he cannot account for anything that happens in his life in terms of his freedom of the will. He invents fate or destiny, but still clinging to his own conception of the self as a separate individual entity endowed with free will, the individual will is obviously a force attached to every thought of doing something. As such it is simply a function of the 'acquired' mind into which one is conditioned. And one's identity, the sense of mineness, which is seen as the origin of one's actions, is itself a part of that acquired mind. And, further, it is obvious that anything acquired through one's upbringing cannot be definitive of the self. The self is prior to all that it experiences.

This is the crux of the matter. There can be no freedom in the system of mind, comprising of thoughts based in memories, which we have acquired and with which we identify ourselves. Or to put it simply, there is no freedom in being the empirical self of which we are constantly conscious of and through which all our experiences are channelised. So the self that we are constantly in touch with, at the empirical level, is a mechanical system, a conditioned apparatus like a computer, with all the laws of its operation built into it. Consciousness can be compared to the common space which we all share. We can build walls around us, sit inside and call it 'my space'. But the space doesn't become yours; demolish the walls and 'your' space merges in the space. It is like the air we breathe. All air on earth is connected. We breathe in and out the same air. Though we can say 'my breath', but not 'my air'. The same applies to the empirical self. "My self" is like "my breath". It is clearly an aspect of the self-consciousness. The "my" is added later to it, by reference to the wall of the body built around it. Give up the empirical identity and the individual self-consciousness merges in the universal consciousness. And here the question of freedom makes a strange turn. If the empirical self is a product of time and social conditioning then spiritual freedom cannot be conceived as freedom of the self in exercising choices as it wishes. Rather, spiritual freedom must be a freedom 'from' the self, that is the acquired self. It must be an ascendance into a timeless, non-social consciousness – a consciousness which is not man-made. Conversely, attachment to the acquired self is the factor of bondage.

We approach life through clamours of attachment and we approach the desire of becoming through glamours of pleasure. And both these modes of being are driven by a tremendous sense of insecurity. In fact both, attachment and becoming, are illusions because they are hopeless means of securing or feeling security. They are hopeless, because attachment is always threatened with frustration and pleasures are always ephemeral. Pleasure indeed gives one a sense of well-being and power. But since it is based in sensations, it is always dependent on external conditions. Pleasure is inherently hollow and hungry for 'more'. It is never self-sufficient and therefore always insecure. The same is true of attachment. Indeed the very search for security in the psychological world, which is determined by pure chance, itself shows the irrationality and unintelligence of the conditional mind. The unself-sufficient, the ephemeral, the dependent can never be secure. So in so far as the individual acquired self shares these characteristics, it can never be secure. And it follows, therefore, that its search for security in life is a grand illusion. But the irony is that it is condemned to this illusion. It is condemned because, as we noted above, both attachment and becoming are anchored in the great primeval fear of "non-being". And this fear arises when thought operating upon being divides it into subject and object of consciousness and perceives the perpetual demise of the subject. Consciousness, hooked to the being of a subject, as opposed to its object, is perpetually disturbed, insecure and fearful. The self which identifies itself with this subject, therefore, is naturally insecure as much. And this gives us the family tree of the bondage we are trying to understand.

We are saying that the human bondage consists in the fact that man is condemned to live in illusion. Thinking that pleasure and attachment will make him secure, he seeks them tirelessly, without realising that up the tree, they are anchored in the fear of non-being. And the fear itself exists due to ignorance of one's own true nature, the nature of being a wave in the ocean of being consciousness-bliss. So the true self-knowledge must reach out up to the essence or ground of one's individual being – all the way up the family tree, from experience to the primordial essence in pure being consciousness.

We can now see the true nature of bondage to the world. It is not just a matter of developing some bad habits and being bound to them, bad as they are no doubt, but behind the day-to-day empirical bondage to desires, there is the whole question of their rootedness in the human condition which props up the individual self-consciousness trampled by the fear of non-being and the demands of becoming. The point at which this happens is when thought divides the wholeness of being-consciousness into a subject and its object, and identifies the subject as a self which is deemed to remain constant throughout a series of experiences. At this point the free and boundless consciousness engaged in its absolute creativity falls in the trap of seeing itself as numerous selves separated from each other by thought in a single stream of time. It is ironical because thought is also a form of consciousness. But as it leaps upon itself, dividing reality, gives birth to numerous selves in the form of subjects of different scenes of experiences. It is ironical because each self sees itself as separate from each other and from total stream of consciousness to which it inalienably belongs. The story of bondage begins from here. Metaphysically speaking, the human bondage consists in the fact that each one of us has to be an individual separated from being and limited in time and its operations by causality. The human spirit is condemned to be its embodiment. Having to be thus and so, he has to do such and such, being ignorant of both his origin and destination. The sensitive mind perceives this bondage and longs for freedom from it.

We can see now that the bondage stipulated exists broadly at two different levels of our existence. One, the familiar day-to-day level of 'perception-desire-intention-will and action'. Thought puts all these into our life. It is the life of memories as we have seen, lived within the operations of attachment and becoming a life of ambition, hopes and frustrations, fuelled by hidden unconscious motives and fears. It is a life of relationship with the world through people, things and the ideas we have about how they should be – the ideals we hold. We believe in various "issues", religions and superstitions. They create the kind of culture we live in, and culture, in turn, shapes the biological man into 'human' beings. The human being is in bondage to his beliefs, because they determine his large choices of life. But more importantly, insidiously, they determine the way we 'feel' about life – our emotions and commitments. Even the very perception of life, which distils through the concepts we have settled for us, is thoroughly conditioned from the start. We scuttle around within a fixed framework but never withdraw and stand apart to have a fresh look at life. We make painful adjustments with it and suffer through it. In the name of 'survival' and 'necessity' we are completely subservient to the 'conditioned'.

But all this can change if we realise, as we have noted, that consciousness has the capacity of simultaneous awareness of what is thrust upon us and of this as a 'fact' that such and such is thrust upon us. In other words, consciousness, in total attention, has the capacity to reject the 'forced' demands of the unconscious silently and without effort and accept only what is necessary for a happy creative living. It is obvious that for this aspect of consciousness as attention to ourselves, to take hold of ourselves, we have to be attentive or watch ourselves, not in separate isolated meditations, but as engaged in day-to-day life – we have to catch ourselves red-handed as it were. What this means is that we have to be open to understanding our relationships with the world that is, we have to be "open" in the sense that, we watch ourselves in action with the intention of understanding only, without any "further" motive of improving our spiritual status, by seeing in direct perception, the basis or ground of our responses in relationship to the world. We want to be exposed to ourselves to see why we behave the way we behave – what is the underlying structure of motives, intentions and beliefs that drag us into reacting the way we do.

Such understanding or knowledge of ourselves is not a matter of specialised psychology. Any one who is attentive to his ordinary behaviour in day-to-day life without being 'judgmental', emotional and assertive about it, will know himself directly. He will realise what real motives, beliefs and ambitions are making him live his life the way he lives. And this knowledge of oneself will be immensely valuable because psychologically it is 'transformative'. It works in the following manner:

Firstly, in the light of this non-cognitive, simultaneous awareness of oneself, one discovers one's real motives, intentions and desires, which are normally camouflaged in the garb of sociability. Normally, when one is absorbed in giving shape to one's desires etc., this non-cognitive self-awareness, that is the simultaneous awareness of the fact that one is behaving thus and so, is not simply a silent watcher of what one is doing. Unconsciously, it is taking stock of what one is doing in a judgmental way – encouraging or discouraging, justifying or decrying one's actions. So the real motive remains hidden to oneself. But consciousness has the capacity to watch itself 'silently', simultaneously to its engagement in the world. And when it does that then the truth about oneself is revealed. It is a meditation which one can be doing most of the time when one is engaged in daily activities, and even when one is analysing thoughts. Of course, it requires an intense passion to know oneself without any further motive of self-advancement.

Now, what one discovers in this kind of self-revelation is that all our efforts to achieve this and that particular successes can be put under same more general headings such as: desire to achieve "powers", "recognition", "wealth" and "social status". This applies to seeking 'knowledge' and 'artistic creation' as well. In all this the mode of living is completely different from that which persists when you live simply "for the love of life". Indeed a great artist or a scientist would from time to time create what he does simply for the love of his art or science. But even he, like the other mediocres, when taken in the context of life as a whole, has the hidden desire for 'glory' if not for riches, for the day when he can say in his heart (or perhaps to his wife) that at last he has achieved something great, something for which he will be remembered by successive generations.

All successes in achievements of various kinds generate a sense of security and create an illusion of safety and permanence. But one longs for it. Isn't it because one is permanently, psychologically insecure? One gathers "more" of everything hoping that he will be secure. But this inner insecurity is not circumstantial, is not due to lack of 'more'.

In fact, the more one has the more one feels the insecurity. There is something primeval about it. It doesn't disappear by having more of power, recognition and so on. Gathering does not stop, nor does the insecurity. And here, if one remains with this feeling without trying to race it out, bravely facing it, then one sees clearly that it is rooted in the primordial fear of non-being. And this fear of non-being, as we noted earlier, in turn, is rooted in the human condition itself. It is the condition when 'thought', seeing the nature of the self as consciousness, finds it without substance and perpetually disturbed, ending in its rising. This state of consciousness is unbearable. One is afraid and like a drowning man clinches every straw it can grab.

The perception of the self as insubstantial and relative to the occurrent states of consciousness produces great fear of life, of continuing without seeking to bestow upon it some sense of permanence. One creates the belief that there is something permanent underneath, though he can't perceive it. A paradoxical state is set.

3

The Self

I think it will be generally agreed that the 'stuff' which constitutes the self includes all my experiences from the early childhood till temporal death. These experiences are retained in memories, while the individual conscious states fall as they rise. So it seems safe to say that the self is a bundle of memories. Indeed this much was said by the famous empiricist philosopher, John Locke, who thought that my self existed "as far back as my memories went" and thus referred to memory as the criterion of the identity of a person overtime.

But there was a problem in this approach. Normally, we think that memory pre-supposes personal identity. That is, commonsense believes that the person or the self whose memories are in question must already exist and have an experience before he can subsequently remember it. So, the self cannot be equated with the bundle of memories, even though the latter does provide the existential 'content' of the self.

In fact, the problem is simply that we normally think of the self as somehow actively involved in making the "bundle" in the first place. A sequence of experiences by themselves do not make a bundle. As we have said, they fall as they rise. And a heap of bricks do not make a structure. So normally we believe that it is the integrating power of self-awareness that converts them into memories and unites them in a single mind.

Another important philosopher, in fact regarded as the father of modern Western philosophy, Rene Descartes, identified the self with the entire mind, which he considered to be a substance. Each person is an individual mental substance which is non-spacial and so completely different from the material substance. Descartes thought that he did not face the problem of personal identity, since all the separate mental states already belonged to one individual thing in virtue of simply being modifications within that substance. The modifications already belong to one mind because the mind of an individual is already a separate individual substance. However, Descartes faced the problem of 'individuation'. Since minds have no physical attributes and they do not occupy space, it is hard to see how one such substance could be distinguished from the other.

Moreover, it is also doubtful if being modification of one substance will be sufficient for separate mental states to belong to one mind. As we have said above, it is the integrating power of self-awareness that brings them together. In ordinary experience we see that the quality of self-awareness is present, at least subliminally, at each instance of a mental state arising in an individual. The "I" accompanies all our mental states. So there is a sense of 'ownership' of all the mental states which the self goes through.

It is this aspect of "mineness" or the sense of "ownership" of mental states that serves as the active agency involved in putting them together into one mind. Both Locke and Descartes missed this point. That is, the idea that the self is all the mental states of an individual taken together doesn't explain how the individual states of one mind enter into that 'unity of mind'. And secondly, they also don't explain how or where the sense of "me" or "mineness" comes into being. This sense of "me" or the ego is so unique that it cannot itself be treated as a mental state among other mental states. Moreover, it accompanies all the mental states. And one specific mental state accompanying all others is simply unintelligible.

This point about the role of self-awareness integrating all other mental states into one mind is very important for a theory of self-knowledge. For self-knowledge, whatever else it may be, must consist in understanding the nature and structure of the self. Now, a structure is not a heap. So understanding the mind of an individual would involve understanding how the mind is structured and what agency is involved in giving it that structure. And understanding the nature of the self would involve how one element in the structure effects the performance of other elements. So a total self-knowledge would require one to know if there is an agency involved in putting all the mental states of an individual into one mind and thus giving the individual a mental identity.

With the above explanations in mind, I think we are now in a position to grasp the nature of the self in its entirety. First of all, there is no denying that the permanent self in all of us is perennially a "subject" and never an "object". Consciousness in its entire career as an experiencer never bumps into an object called "the self". However, the self-consciousness, which is conceptualised and represented by the term "I", comes into existence at every stance of a perception by the self. It comes into existence in the response of "thought" to the perceptions in question. The subject – self, on having a perception, immediately responds to it by its own power of thought. In this response it divides the natural unity of the subject and its perception into the perceiving-self and its perceived object. The perennial subject self thus, on the one hand, turns itself into a conceptualised self, subsumed under the concept of an individual entity, the "I", and on the other, puts its perception at an objective distance as an object perceived by the "I". The subject—self—in its own eternal nature as a creative consciousness does not know itself until it objectifies itself in thought, as an "I". But it is important to note that, obviously, what it knows now to be the subject, namely the "I", is only a conceptualised version of the real self, which never sheds its status as the subject. The real self, which in our spiritual literature is normally written with a capitol "S", is eternally absorbed in its creativity. But thought, which is an off-shoot of its creativity, creates a conceptualised self-awareness or self-consciousness, which follows upon the original subject—consciousness—so swiftly that we do not even notice the moment of the birth of "I-consciousness".

In his philosophy of Non-Dualism, Shankara defines the original reality of the creative self as being-consciousness. How right he is! Being is never by itself nor is consciousness. It is only in response of thought that being is objectified and separated from its creative consciousness.

So the truth that emerges after the above explanation appears to be this: In day-to-day life what we call "self-awareness" is not the awareness of the true self but only the concept-self. And the integrating power of self-awareness which I have talked about above, manifests its integration only in thought. No wonder, our mind is "given" as an organised system of concepts. And reality is always perceived through these concepts.

In the traditional spiritual philosophy, the difference between the self and the individual self or the ego is most important. Because, as we can see now, that we live with the conceptual self, the "I", and in day-to-day life confuse it with the real self. It is the "I" that organises all our experiences and puts them into a single mind, which constitutes, what we have called the 'stuff' of the self, in philosophy called the "empirical self".

The first step in self-knowledge, therefore, must be taken at the level of the empirical self, exploring its internal connections and through that coming to an understanding of the nature of the "I". It is only then that we can come to see it as a false entity, created by the response of thought to reality. Only then, again, we may be in actual fact able to shed it and remain established in our true nature as the eternally creative being-consciousness, which Shankara rightly sees as blissful. Creativity has no inner conflicts and therefore naturally blissful. Further, being free from the "I", it is timeless and rightly deserves the title "transcendental". What it transcends is the duality of the division between "I" and not "I" which is typical of the empirical reality. For the same reason it also exemplifies the state of 'spiritual freedom', which is a freedom from the self into the creative consciousness of the true self.

We can now sum up the reflections so far.

In ordinary life each one of us is aware of himself as "being thus and so". This ordinary awareness of the self has two components, one of "being" and the other of "thus and so". Consciousness of 'being' is not conscious of an 'object'. It is an intuitive awareness of existence. Existence is not a descriptive notion and can't be analysed any further. A thing either has this awareness or does not. Human beings have this awareness of "being-consciousness" before they acquire the second component of "being thus and so". The latter is a learnt identity added to the intuitive being-consciousness which has no reference to time, place or form. Being-consciousness is at the core of individual existence and it is a timeless phenomenon. How and when it comes to be associated with a particular empirical biography is a deep mystery. We will make an attempt to understand this mystery. But the mystery is solved only in enlightenment or in complete self-knowledge.

In total meditative self-awareness it would be realised that at the core of selfhood there is simply 'being consciousness'. Being consciousness is known intuitively. Everyone knows, without observation, what it is to be in the world and what it is to be conscious. If 'consciousness' were a learnt concept, it would have its empirical counterpart – something which another person could point out and say that 'it is consciousness' or at least that 'it is a manifestation of consciousness. But there is no such phenomenon. It is because we are born with this intuitive understanding of consciousness that we are able to recognise the difference between conscious beings and non-conscious being in the first place. Moreover, if consciousness were not conscious of itself intrinsically, nothing will ever make it self-conscious, since it is not objectively present. It will remain unconscious of itself and consequently, it will remain unconscious of the world. The latter is so because consciousness sees the world only as it is 'revealed' to itself, i.e. in self-consciousness.

We do not experience consciousness as such. We experience objects of consciousness. And simultaneously to experiencing an object, we become aware of the presence of consciousness non-cognitively. Thus, for example, I see a rose flower and simultaneously to my seeing – experience, I also become aware of the fact that I see the rose. That is I become self-aware. Sometimes I may not be conscious of the fact in question, if I am deeply absorbed in my experience of seeing the rose, but subliminally the awareness of the fact of seeing the rose is present. It lurks in the background, and I can easily summon it. This non-cognitive awareness of consciousness is what Shankara and others have described as 'self-luminosity' of consciousness or 'intuitive knowledge' of the presence of consciousness. Similar observations are made with regard to the intuition of 'being'. That is, it is because we know what it is to 'be' already that we are able to recognise the presence of different kinds of being and distinguish between individual beings in the first place.

Now, the "being consciousness" must be clearly distinguished from "individuality-consciousness". Being-consciousness per se has no individuality. The latter is acquired during the process of growth and evolution in the world. Obviously, since for recognising oneself as an individual self, I must be able to distinguish myself from other selves. That is, I must be able to recognise myself as 'I-this, I-that'. That is, I must ascribe to myself properties which are unique to me. In regular life, the only properties which are unique to me are memories of past experience. If we observe carefully, from the very infancy, perhaps from before we are born, we become aware of the kinaesthetic sensations of our bodies. And with them we construct a mental image of ourselves as occupying a spatially extended object, i.e. the body, in the psychological space. This gives the primary identity of individuality-consciousness. I begin to see myself as "I-this", that is, I-the body occupying the space constituting the kinaesthetic sensations. So far my individuality is not defined in terms of any social properties. But as I live, and start growing into certain basic relationships, such as with parents and my immediate environment I begin to enter the constitution of my individual identity. The memories of these basic relationships form the core of my individual identity together with my already constructed bodily identity. I make a mental image of this identity and call it 'myself'. This constitutes my empirical or psychological self. There is no such thing as the intuition of pure individual "I". There cannot be. The "I" must be distinguished from "non-I's" and other "I's". For this, the "I" must ascribe properties to itself. That is, it must, from the start, be "I-this, I-that". That is, the individuality is an acquired thing. Individuality is built upon the eternal and universal core element of 'being consciousness', which must be clearly distinguished from individual self-consciousness. Being conscious is simply the 'ground' upon which individual self-consciousness is erected. The individual self-consciousness is the 'solid' entity made of mental things. As explained above, this 'solid' entity, the mental self, solidified, as it were, by its own logic of interdependent – origination in kinaesthetic sensations, has the potentiality of carrying on even after physical death of a person, paving the way for belief in rebirth.

Direct Knowledge

This point about the response of thoughts to reality is very important. It can be generalised as follows. The response of thought to reality – in which the ego comes into existence – is always "separative". Thought isolates a fragment of reality and makes a concept of it. In this way, the world is presented to consciousness as "conceptualised". And we loose direct contact with reality.

In the pursuit of self-knowledge, it is important to bear in mind. Self-knowledge is not the conceptualised knowledge of the "self". It will be objected at the moment that all knowledge is only a matter of forming concepts of reality. But this cannot be strictly true. For, before a concept is formed of some segment of reality, your direct contact with it must tell you something about it for you to form a concept of it in the first place. There is indeed such a thing as 'knowing directly' without the interference of a concept. But it is not easy to describe the nature of this knowledge. It seems to melt away in a kind of being. For example, if I am directly aware of my fear, without a word or interpretation, its true nature is revealed in my becoming that fear itself. When the gap between me and the 'object' fear is filled in direct contact with it, the fear as an object separate from me seems to disappear – it becomes a part of "being-in-continuous transformation". The knowledge which is always objectified, separated from being is quite different from direct knowledge.

Now, from the above considerations, it will not be speculative to infer that the self of which we are aware in self-awareness, the familiar "I" cannot be some kind of substantial entity, which is capable of independent existence, either physical or mental. Rather, it is a complex entity, a mental image, constructed over a period of time, of which we are unconscious, in which a number of ego-states are critically coalesced, arising, as we have seen in the response of thought to reality. That is, there is a largely unconscious nucleus of the self-image which is strengthened and modified as life goes on, and which is constantly present at every new perception. It is this image what we refer to by the word "I" and mistakenly take it to be a simple mental substance remaining one and the same throughout our rapidly changing biography. I say 'mistakenly', because, as we have seen, it is really conceptual, born in the response of thought to reality.

Perhaps we can see this process of self-creation more clearly if we consider an example of an actual perception. Suppose I see a bush of roses in front of me. Now, at the moment of the contact of consciousness with the bush, there is no division of the seer and the seen – there is only the unity of being-consciousness. But as soon as thought apprehends it, it says: I see a bush of roses. Thought has then drawn a wedge between the seer and the seen. The seer has been conceptualised as the "I" or the subject and the seen is a 'bush of roses'. In this way, on each occasion of a perception a subject-I is separated from the object seen. And many such images of the subject-I are spliced together to form the self which becomes the reference point of origination of all the mental activity of an individual person. But in this picture, it is clear that the self created psychologically is conceptual; the real self as consciousness which originally comes in contact with the reality of the bush is not captured by thought. It remains the subject of 'all' consciousness, before the division by thought, and never becomes an object in the world.

We can see here that the response of thought to reality, in one go, cerates both the individual self or the 'I', and the world as apprehended under concepts. Both the world and the self are then in a sense only conceptual realities. We will have more to say about the logical status of conceptual realities later. For the present I will only mention that in the traditional rendition both these are said to be created by the divine power of *Maya*. "*Maya*" literally means 'to measure'. We can see that the sages have rightly conceived 'concepts' as the measure of reality. It is only by applying concepts that we determine the epistemic status of objects as "real" or "illusory", and also we measure their ultimate ontic reality.

So any approach to self-knowledge must take into account the enormous difference between the empirically created self and the self-existent, eternal subject-self. And from the religious and spiritual point of view, it must realise that the understanding of the nature and structure of the self is not an end in itself – it is a way of coming to see the conceptual, and in that sense the illusory, nature of the self, in order to end the separation of the "I-self" from the self.

My attachment is with my body of which I am constantly conscious, from the inside, through kinaesthetic sensations, and my consciousness of my body in this way is my mental image of myself. And I am attached to this image and through it with my personal world. I am not attached to my **real self** of which I am not conscious objectively. I am that real self which is eternally present by its own power. So my self-awareness, in the empirical world, is a sheer illusion.

Self-knowing in the full sense puts one in touch with one's "authentic self". If a person can put aside all that he has learnt about himself throughout his upbringing – his name and form and accumulations etc. – he will be still left with something at the centre of his being. This something is his sense of existing, his "sense of presence". This sense of presence is without any boundaries, without any location, etc. It is simply "being-consciousness". Without this sense he will simply be another 'object' in the world of objects, wholly explicable in terms of physics. But he is not that. His being-consciousness signifies a quality of life which is "non-computational". It signifies universal presence and pure-consciousness. The latter notion has to be taken with care. It does not mean "consciousness without an object". Consciousness always has some object internal to it. The notion of "pure consciousness" means consciousness without individual ego i.e. ego with an acquired identity. All creative consciousness is without ego. But consciousness is always aware, subliminally as it were, of its creativity. It is a form of self-consciousness, signifying the presence of the universal self. Above all, this being-consciousness is permeated with the bliss of love. Love is a sense of "the unity of being". It is all inclusive. There is no division or a 'sense of separation' in it. So the authentic self can be seen as made of love, which is not seeking anything, which is not desire but pure creativity. Thus, we can see, that the empirical self or the ego, at its nucleus, is one with the universal self or the absolute creative consciousness. The empirical self is an instance of the pure consciousness wrapped up in an identity. It is indeed like a wave in the ocean.

The Nature of Self-Knowledge

In the earlier sections we have seen that though each of us necessarily possesses self-awareness, we do not possess its knowledge as such. This is because the self-disclosed in self-awareness is of a very vague and general kind. First, at the transcendental level, we have an intuition of its presence which is anchored in pure 'being-consciousness'. And this consciousness does not suggest that the self is a separate individual entity. The self melts into nothingness as it were into a timeless and universal presence of a blissful consciousness which is limitless. Then, at the empirical level, self-awareness discloses the nature of the self non-cognitively only as the subject of all one's cognitive, conative and volitional experiences. We have seen how at this level self-consciousness arises as a response of thought to the original 'primitive' consciousness of the world, which splits consciousness into a subject and its object. But the ontological reality of this subject is not disclosed in this awareness. The self, i.e. the existential self, is perennially a subject whose only identity is determined by reference to what it holds as 'object'. Again, introspectively, this self is not revealed as a separate individual entity. And logically, from the fact that we possess such a consciousness of 'separateness', it does not follow that in reality there is actually such an entity – an "I" which remains one and the same throughout its varying biography. We have seen how this consciousness of separateness arises in response of thought only. But before and beyond thought, the nature of pure consciousness (i.e. consciousness without an 'I') remains unknown. Consciousness per se, which seems to be the substance of the self, prior to becoming consciousness of separate existence, remains in the background as a 'limitless absolute', unknowable by thought. As the sages tell us, it is knowable only in pure intuition when the consciousness of separateness, the 'I', has been shed in transcendence of the empirical self. So the knowledge of the self in completeness must culminate in the knowledge of this ground reality of the 'limitless absolute'. A complete self-knowledge, therefore, must include the knowledge of the empirical self, the "I" with its consciousness of separateness, together with the mechanism of its emergence, traced back in the ground reality. The knowledge of the empirical or the existential self, the "I", can only be acquired operationally, by observing it function in day-to-day relationship in the world. But the knowledge of its ground in the limitless absolute must be a higher spiritual achievement. Man can hope to reach this highest reality of one's own being since there is a link to it from thought to it. And the link there must be because thought has originated from it and also has to return to it. So the complete picture of self-knowledge is highly complex – from thought to the absolute pure consciousness.

However, the fact that the self which we 'live out' and suffer or enjoy is always present as the subject of all our experiences gives us a vital clue as to how we can know it in the proper sense of "knowledge". It tells us that we can know it "operationally" – in the whole structure of its active relationship with its objects. Surely, to an acute observer even the unconscious aspects of this relationship must be manifest in every experience considered as a whole.

Furthermore, we can see that this type of self-knowledge is not just a theoretical matter. Like in all cases of scientific first-hand knowledge, one has first to confront the phenomenon to be known which in this case can be inwardly perceived linked as: perception-desire-intention-leading to action. So in this case, the self has to be perceived in actual operation in real life. To know oneself as a subject of experiences, one has to confront oneself in awareness of all one's relationships – which amounts to living in total awareness of what is going on in one's life, with all its hidden motives and expectations. And now one can see that this awareness of oneself-in-action has to be pure watchfulness, without the imposition of an interpretation or pre-conceived ideas of what is going on. Fortunately, we have this non-cognitive power of silent watchfulness, of witnessing, what is going on within our own consciousness, without interfering with it. The non-cognitive aspect of consciousness, which we have identified in cognitive processes, has to be completely silent without the interferences of our conditioned mind. Surely, if the 'hidden, the unconscious is to reveal itself, we have to receive it with untainted consciousness.[1]

(Attention is a form of that type of consciousness). In attention one has a sense of "being present", without the confines of temporality – a sense of presence without the measurements of concepts. All human actions are motivated. The motives are normally hidden from the surface consciousness. But in the organised mind of a human being they are manifestations of some fundamental traits of human existence. At the deepest level this trait is of the form of "desire to continue" both psychologically and physically. The latter is happening in the concrete form as the continuity of the body with which we identify ourselves. Indeed the body is changing all the time according to the laws of physics. But there is a sense of continuity of the 'same' body, because the changes are imperceptible and the perception of the kinaesthetic sensations of the body is constantly carried over by memory during sleep. As noted earlier, mentally we are aware of our embodiedness in the form of our occupancy of

1. Cf J. Krishnamurti's notion of 'Choiceless Awareness".

the psychological space with which we consciously identify the physical body.

But the psychological continuity is seriously threatened. Mainly this is so because consciousness by its very nature is perpetually disturbed. And also because we frequently lose the consciousness of continuity, for example in deep sleep or when we are absorbed in some creative activity or generally, when we are inattentive to our activities. Not finding perpetual continuity, perhaps, we invent a permanent individual soul which gives an underlying, though imperceptible, continuity. Whatever may be the truth in this matter, it remains undeniable that individual states of consciousness are rapidly changing. And secondly, because self-consciousness under the title "I" provides only an empty "form" for substantial existence. The "I" needs to be defined by an identity – it needs to 'become' something substantial, as it were. But consciousness cannot literally become matter, a "thing", with computational qualities. So it acquires psychological labels as "I-this", "I-that" etc. The "I" being empty in itself must determine itself as the possessor, the owner of such and such attributes. It finds such attributes under the titles of 'rich', 'famous', 'powerful', 'talented', 'learned' etc. In this way a process of "becoming" is set in, at the psychological level of one's existence. So the fundamental parameters of the human condition can be set out in terms of (1) "the disturbed consciousness" and (2) "the desire to continue". These, as we explore later, are two fundamentals "structures" of the self. The third being "attachment". For the present, let us note that it is these traits of the human condition that produce the entire motivational structure of human existence. Self-knowledge, therefore, must involve an upward understanding of the fundamental focus of the human condition and the entire motivational structure of existence that flows from them. We have, therefore, to understand how the human condition realised itself in actual life and how it determines our individual modes of existence.

The Perpetually Disturbed Consciousness

What we are describing as "perpetually disturbed consciousness" in fact points to its nature as perpetually creative. At the empirical level, the individual consciousness is manifested within the framework of time, space and causality. But the consciousness, which creates the framework itself, which is immersed in absolute creativity, which has no beginning and no end, is beyond any limitations. It is a movement of spontaneity of life itself. Such a movement can't be 'stable', static or confined. The absolute creativity which is timeless in itself is apprehended by us as manifest within the world of thought. And in the world of thought it is perpetually disturbed and broken up in the sense that seen through temporality and quality it appears ephemeral. The individual consciousness sees it fall as it rises from its temporal. Being unaware of its identity with the infinite and eternal flow of life itself, it is fearful of the temporal. The consciousness, which is perpetually disturbed, which is ephemeral, is condemned to seek a sense of permanence in life. Life, which is moment-to-moment new in its creativity, is feared for its death in temporality. The individual self needs an anchorage in time. So it creates a sense of permanence in relationships. The most important mechanism to achieve this sense is through bonds of "attachments". It hold those shifting identities of itself through memories bound with psychological states of attachments. Psychologically the individual tries to feign ignorance of the fact that all relationships, either with people or with things, are in reality impermanent. But through attachments, generating a sense of "mineness", it thinks that it has assimilated the object related to, in its very being. Thus memory through attachments creates a sense of permanence in relationships. The thought-consciousness is, therefore, constantly falsifying reality. Attachments create an illusion of permanence. Self-knowledge destroys this 'illusion pertaining to the permanence of the individual self as a separate existent by exposing that its attachments signal the wrong 'truth'. In self-knowledge, that is, in the knowledge, as we have said, of the operational self, one realises that one really belongs to the whole world – that one is connected with the whole of existence in an inseparable way. The operational self would not come to exist without those connections, in the sense that one is not 'detachable' from them like the parts of a machine. Let us see more vividly how this picture of the 'whole' stands.

First, at the physical level these connections within a whole are so obvious. The body is made of the elements which get into him from "outside" of him. And in order to sustain life, the individual must be in constant touch with the world, through breath and other forms of energy. But, psychologically, one might say, it appears that the individual self is a separate entity. The mind of the individual is a self-enclosed entity, cut-off from other similar entities. But a quick reflection upon the fact of how a mind is formed demolishes this myth. From the early childhood, in order to acquire a mind, the individual has to struggle learning a language, acquiring concepts and developing a sense of meaning. We all know the story of wolf-children who remained without minds as they were deprived of social interaction. The capacity to think and remember will remain dormant without interaction within the 'whole'.

So self-knowledge tells you the truth that the individual self-hood is constructed out of the materials in a reality which exists independently of the individual's will. And as we have seen in the earlier chapter, when one deconstructs oneself by putting aside all the accumulated memories etc., one is left with only the ground of the self-hood which is universal being-consciousness.

4

The Primordial Fear

The most significant aspect of the human condition is the primeval "fear of non-being". This fear of non-being is primeval because it is connected with the nature of consciousness itself. Consciousness in its very nature is fundamentally creative. Being creative it is vested with spontaneity. It arises without a 'cause' and exists by constantly changing itself in creativity. So it is perpetually disturbed. It is a moment to moment creative existence.

Now, at the empirical level, to a limited ego-centred human consciousness, this form or mode of existence of consciousness appears to be perpetually threatened by death. In this way, a primordial fear of non-being is set in. The human consciousness, squashed between 'time' and 'causality', manifests this fear continually in day-to-day living in a variety of ways. He needs to be highly sensitive to notice the changing faces of this fear. In day-to-day life he hides, suppresses and tries to avoid facing it. In its gross form it manifests as fear of physical death. But in its more sophisticated forms it creeps into every fold of life in a variety of ways. Read how a contemporary mystic philosopher puts it, "Most of us have fears: fear of the doctor, fear of disease, fear of not achieving, fear of being left alone, fear of old age, fear of poverty; these are outward fears. Then there are a thousand and one inward fears: the fear of public opinion, of death, of being left completely alone so that you have to face life without a companion, the fear of loneliness, the fear of not reaching what you call God. So man has a thousand and one fears. And being frightened, he either escapes in a vast network, subtle or crude, or he rationalises these fears; or he becomes neurotic, because he cannot understand it, he cannot resolve it, or he completely runs away from fear, from various fears, through identification of social activities, reformation joining a political party and so on". (KFI, 1992, To Live With Death, J. Krishnamurti, p. 6)

Now, any moderately rational person can see that a life lived in constant fear would be intrinsically worthless. Indeed such a life lends itself very easily to evil and wickedness. It is a well-known perception, that an animal, for example, attacks you only if he is himself afraid of you. That is why, some well known saints and enlightened beings, like Raman Maharshi, could walk with hunting animals unharmed by them – these saints did not evoke any fear in the animal. Another well-known piece of psychology is that the viciousness of hard criminals is their protective response to deal with the immense "insecurity" which they suffer in their hearts. We also know that fear breeds anxiety and in some cases actually kills the fearful. By suppressing his fear the person potentially becomes more violent. Such a person is a serious danger to "harmony" in the society. And for oneself it becomes a source of numerous psychosomatic diseases.

So it is essential to eradicate fear from our hearts. How shall we do it? Perhaps when a person becomes completely neurotic, some outside help of a psychiatrist might help. But as we have said the fears are constantly present in everyone's life. In day-to-day life, and mostly unconsciously, we are all driven to escape or react from our fears. In such a situation our human relationships are bound to become degenerate.

Instead of relating to each other in love, trust and friendship, we are bound to be aggressive, suspicious and uncaring.

All over the world, the religious approach is "prayers". But ordinary prayer is a mechanical exercise, it is flattery and driven by greed. It is very doubtful if God will be moved by such attempts. Only a massive shower of God's grace could pull one out of this situation. But one has to be deserving to receive such a shower.

Krishnamurti himself suggests that each one of us has to bring to an end this fear by his own effort by confronting them in a state of "choiceless awareness". In this way you are in "direct" contact with fear, not through an idea of it.

In this state you face your fear without trying to escape from it in some pleasant activity. Nor, do you react to it in any manner. A simple effortless watchfulness without yielding to it at all is sufficient to get rid of the fear. Try it and see for yourself if it works. I find that it does. But the trouble with this kind of exercise is that, as Krishnamurti himself notes, there are a thousand and one fears'. Even in a life time one cannot get through them all one by one.

Surely, to understand and thus go beyond fear, one has to, as Krishnamurti says, be in "direct" contact with fear. But it seems to me that this contact has to be established at the 'source' and not with particular fears. The source is the origin of 'all' fears and we have seen that it is the primordial fear of non-being. Now, at what point does this fear arise? Clearly, in the original reality of the unity of being and consciousness there is no fear: The transcendental-being as the subject of 'all' consciousness, is eternally immersed in its universal creativity. But, as we have seen, the response of thought splits the original unity of being-consciousness into numerous temporal subjects. This temporal subject, the individual self, then, apprehending its time-bound existence, naturally becomes frightened of its fatality.

So the source we are looking for is there – it is the moment of the arising of individual selves in the response of thought to reality. The individual self, centred in a point of self-awareness as subject, separated from the object it holds in consciousness, isolates itself from the universal being-consciousness. In this isolation it is fearful of its moment to moment demise, and, as we have seen longs to "become" something definite and continue for ever, as it were. So the primordial fear is born with the birth of the individual self's consciousness of itself. So as long as the self-awareness delivers individuality and separateness from the universal being, it is difficult to see how the primordial fear can be got rid off.

To destroy this fear, obviously, the answer is a return to the universal unity of being, that is, only when the individual self is merged with the higher self, the fear automatically drops out. That is why, the merger of the self with the higher self is the goal in all the religions of Indian origin, as well as of the non-theistic spiritual systems of meditation. First, one has to come to see the insubstantial nature of the individual self. Thought, in the form of memory, has given the self, the status of a permanent being. One believes that one is the same psychological entity, the same individual self, throughout one's temporal existence, in this life and beyond. One believes that this entity is a separate and substantial entity, having its own intrinsically distinct identity. But unconsciously, one knows that the self exists only in states of consciousness as subject relative to the object it perceives. And these states of consciousness are ephemeral. So the permanence of the individual self, and its absolute separateness from them, is an illusion. One sees this truth intellectually. One sees that the individual self exists only in thought. In reality, it is one with the original universal self, which is the subject of all consciousness. But seeing this truth intellectually does not destroy the illusion. One carries on as usual in fear of non-being.

So unless one has an experience of the actual dissolution of the individual self-awareness in a higher consciousness, either of a personal God or of pure being-consciousness, one cannot be free from the illusion in question and its consequent fear.

In the long history of Indian religion, we find a number of saints, yogis and sanyasis, who have attained the dissolution of the self, or its merger with the supreme-self or being-consciousness, respectively, known as "Ishwara" and "Brahman". And the state of merger is called "Samadhi".

The effect of a personal experience of Samadhi is that a saint, when out of Samadhi, though aware of his individuality empirically, is not taken in by the illusion. It is like a desert nomad who knows a mirage for what it is, and does not run to it to quench his thirst. The saint who has realised the truth about the self, experientially, lives out his embodied temporal life as a normal person, with the difference that he no longer lives in fear. The experience of Samadhi has destroyed his primordial fear at the root. So in the empirical situation it does not manifest in particular fears.

How does one get this experience of merger? There doesn't seem to be any straightforward method to attain it. But broadly speaking, those who attain it are passionately and sincerely engaged in discriminative attention to "what is", attaching no or very little value to the pursuit of their personal desires. They attain a stillness of mind in which truth is revealed in a flash. Alternatively, those who believe in a personal God, attain it through long devotion and contemplation of the divine in any of his recognised forms such as of Krishna or Christ. The devotional approach requires, at some point, a total "surrender" to God, again involving a suspension of their personal will with respect to desire fulfilment. And those who do not believe in a personal God, spend their time in meditation upon the attributes of the formless Brahman. However, all the approaches to the ultimate truth require living a totally selfless life accompanied by a personal discipline of body and mind. But in the end, they get into Samadhi, quite spontaneously, when all the conditions of virtue, devotion, meditation or contemplation are rightly fulfilled.

So it would be a gross mistake to think that getting rid of the primeval fear is a matter of being intrepid and facing the challenges of life with full force so as to win over them. It is not a matter of 'conquering' the fear. That is only a mechanism of suppressing it and pushing it deep into the unconscious, from where it remains active in an invisible way.

Look at the many forms of distortions it brings into one's life! Emotionally, every 'conquest' may fill you with pride. It may make you boastful and intolerant. And these contortions are bound to affect your personal relationships adversely. They are bound to turn you into a crooked piece of timber from the inside. And generally, the activity of the unconscious fears put you in a constant battle against personal truths of life. One is always hiding them and trying to present them to others hypocritically and pretentiously.

So by fighting fears there is no hope of winning in the end. Simply, because there just is no end, until you have eradicated it at the very source.

5

The Psychological Becoming

Just as there is primordial fear of non-being, there is also a primordial mechanism of "becoming", that is, the way of retaining being through constant becoming. 'Becoming' should be distinguished from mere 'change'. The latter is embedded in the nature of things. In the entire cosmos everything is constantly changing. So it is in the individual human being. Both his body and mind are witnessing constant changes. But becoming involving self-awareness as a mechanism of hiding the unbearable truth of change is what we are concerned with. Here again, we must make a distinction between 'natural' becoming and 'psychological' becoming. It is natural for a human being to try to attain high standards with respect to the qualities of his natural endowments in talents, skills or intelligence. In this exercise his involvement with his creativity is 'for the love of', for example, his music. On the other hand, he may be playing his music always with an eye on "goods external" to music, such as money, fame, influence and social status etc. The latter are examples of becoming "psychologically", what he is not intrinsically, in his being. His becoming rich or famous is merely an aspect of the social organisation of his time. The existence of things called 'fame' or 'wealth' is a contingent matter. In many older societies they simply did not exist. Anyway the distinction is clear enough. Now what I am suggesting is that "becoming" is a very powerful structure of the self which covers a multitude of sins. In psychological becoming, in contrast with the natural becoming, the individual concerned is not only trying to realise goods external to music, he is also not trying to realise goods internal to his being. That is, he is not aiming at the full realisation of his natural potentialities. Since his eyes are fixed on 'external' gains, he looses the freedom and spontaneity of consciousness, which are necessary conditions for the realisation of inner potentialities. Moreover, since eyes are fixed on 'externals', his happiness is dependent upon success in attaining these things. Such happiness is not true inner happiness – it is second-hand happiness. It does not signify a movement towards the flowering of full humanity in the individual concerned.

The present notion of the "achiever", which is the trade mark of contemporary culture, is stuck to the idea of becoming psychologically – becoming rich, famous, influential, etc. It is a result of a heavy conditioning of the mind. Young people feel proud of being achievers. No doubt some of them portray high standards, but none of them are genuine and authentic in themselves. They cannot be. If they are aiming at goods external to their art and at qualities like aggressiveness and cleverness etc. which are external to their true humanity, then they have already betrayed themselves. They have already lost the perspective of the 'whole', where life has a meaning beyond conditioned success, and creativity is imbued with happiness beyond ordinary human happiness.

Moreover, becoming psychologically is a 'double' illusion. First, since, as we have seen, the empirical self itself is a construct, forced upon pure being-consciousness by the heavy conditioning we undergo during childhood. As such it has no unique and permanent essence as an individual, and in that sense it is unreal ontologically. So to enrich that self psychologically with titles such as "rich" and "famous" can to say the least, only be a foolish activity. And, next, at best it can only be an illusion, since to enrich something which itself has only a circumstantial existence cannot be to add anything real to anything.

Secondly, becoming is an illusion because it doesn't alter your 'human condition' in any way.

Becoming rich, for example, doesn't mean that one can avoid getting old and infirm. It doesn't mean that one can avoid disease and death, when one has to leave all one's richness behind. Nor does it guarantee that if one goes to the operation theatre, one will come out of it alive. In fact, becoming rich is festered with its own problems of anxiety and insecurity over keeping it safe, and keeping oneself safe because of possessing it. Still one likes to become rich, because temporarily it creates a false sense of security. While, in fact, there is no such thing as security, either in one's body or in one's mind. Nor is there security in one's relationships. Every one knows that a thousand promises can be broken if the promisor changes her mind. And any relationship can be lost if the loved one dies suddenly or becomes neurotic under pressure from contingencies of life.

Yet we all cling to the idea of security and seek it all the time in every little thing. Why is that so? One reason is that, as we have seen earlier, we all live under constant fear of non-being. And as we have also seen that this fear can be allayed only by true and complete self-knowledge. Another reason lies, as in the earlier case, with the wrong characterisation of the subject-self. The subject-self, the "I", which is the centre or the reference point of all one's conscious states, has no inner self-identity. The "I" is nothing unless it is seen in relation to its object of consciousness as its subject. The "I" has no unique quality which may give it its specific "me-ness". This inherent emptiness of the "I" is a matter of great concern for self-consciousness. The emptiness of itself is unbearable to the self. It makes it feel most insecure, and it must rush to give itself an identity. It must identify itself with something. But the inner condition of the "I" remains unchanged. So the "I" must keep filling itself continuously till death. Though it knows that it is not able to fill itself permanently, it still continues the process. It does so because engaging in the process itself gives it a false sense of security. It sees no option but to go on securing being through becoming.

But surely, it seems reasonable to suggest that a rational being must give up the false if he sees the falsity in it. If he sees that the sense of security is an illusion then he must stop seeking it. And if he sees that the process of psychological becoming is undertaken in order to feel secure, then he must also stop becoming. In line with this kind of thinking, some spiritual thinkers, notably Krishnamurti, profess that seeing the illusive nature of becoming is sufficient motivation to drop it instantaneously.

This may be true for some. But only for those who are so sensitive to the perception of the 'false' that their whole being is 'shaken up' in reconciliation with the truth. But for the rest of us the effect of this perception is not so deep and it is short-lived. We have to go the whole hog, as it were, and see how this process of becoming sets in in the first place. This will take us to the origin of self-awareness as an individual entity. As in the earlier case of fear, in yogic meditation or in contemplation of the divine, one may wade through one's numerous identities in time, and come upon the experience of consciousness entering 'time' and acquiring an empirical identity as the subject of a particular perception in the objective world. One may catch oneself emerging as a subject relative to an object of perception. And then one may realise that such momentary 'subjects' are held together into an individual self only by memory, as the memory of one momentry subject's self is spliced on to the next. The individual self in itself is insubstantial. It rises and falls like a wave in the ocean of 'all' consciousness. Such experience will be like entering into the state of Samadhi, where the individual self is dissolved into the universal self. How does one get this experience? Again there is no fixed method for this. And the rest of the story is the same as we have explained in the previous section.

The point we are making here is that unless one has the experiential knowledge of the emergence and the dissolution of the individual self, one's self-knowledge is not complete. And for a spiritual transformation to take place we need the complete picture. The complete picture shows how the individual self is not really separate and detachable from the universal self. And this shows that one's sense of insecurity and the need of 'becoming' are futile.

Another complexity in becoming psychologically arises due to the fact that it is always relative to one's idea of what one is at present. What one truly is, either empirically or transcendentally, is normally not accessible to conscious mind. So one makes a mental image of oneself. Everyone has a mental image of oneself largely in terms of one's potentialities and capacities which one tends to realise, selectively, in the process of becoming. Generally people have a 'good' image of themselves unless one is neurotic. There self-image is packed with beliefs about qualities which they may or may not actually possess or at least not in the degree in which they tend to believe. More successful people generally have a very inflated self-image. And most of them are miserable when they don't reach the target. There is a well-known adage which says that "one thinks of oneself in terms of potentialities and of others in terms of their actualities".

When it comes to the moral content of one's self-image, everyone is a good person. There is always virtue at the core of even a hard criminal, which justifies his way of life in his own eyes. We can see clearly then that the self-image inhibits any chance of moral reform or improvement.

So the tragedy of one's life of' 'becoming' is this. Normally, for a sane and good life, our actions should be based on self-knowledge. Without knowing oneself, acting from conditioning, guided by the self-image, will be simply mechanical, lacking any overall purpose and deeper meaning to life. But actions involved in psychological becoming are based only in one's self-image. They are not based even in an empirical self-knowledge, whereas, ideally, they should be based on total self-knowledge, including the knowledge of the transcendental self. This shows that becoming is a doubly false exercise. First, it doesn't even aim at removing the feeling of insecurity false as it is, for which end it is set up in the first place. And two, what it aims at is the fulfilment of the self-image, which itself is an unconscious product of conditioning by the social environment.

We can now sum up the reflections in this section. It is evident enough that from the early days of evolution, man has been geared to become. The needs of biological survival had set in the process of seeking to become this and that, to acquire and invent and to transfer his skills etc. to the younger generation. But in the early stages all his becomings were related to his physical needs and to his basic creative urges. There are cave-paintings depicting games, dancing and music-making. They are all related to his natural instinctive behaviour. It is not clear if he felt sophisticated emotions like 'loneliness' and 'boredom' etc. but he seems to have felt some manifestation of primeval fear, as he is always found in groups, ready often to accept deprivations for the sake of being allowed to live with others. However, with the growth of civilisation, new, culturally crafted, goals became available to him. From now on he was to seek these goals and was applauded and rewarded for successes in them. He doesn't see the logical absurdity of this mode of being: that seeking to become takes it for granted that one is really, in his essence, "a seeking agent". And the absurdity is that without knowing his own reality in essence he is compelled to spend his life in this mode and die without realizing its meaning.

So if one realises that "first thing first" then 'becoming' doesn't come into picture. Becoming has to wait and one has to enter the mode of "seeing what is" for its own sake, and not in order to become enlightened etc., but seeing what life is as it is. And this means that one has to be wholly surrendered and receptive in total attention to 'what is' generally, without focusing one's attention selectively on any particular object (as it is done in some forms of meditation). And also without generating thoughts of being the subject of those attentive states, as one does unconsciously, as we have seen, in empirical self-construction.

In seeking to become, one is taking for granted that one is 'incomplete' in oneself, that one is insecure, and there is a constant need to act to make oneself secure and complete. But on seeing how things really are, how oneself essentially is, this 'launching' belief may turn out to be a mere illusion. For one may find that oneself, being like a wave in the ocean, is already as secure and complete as the ocean is.

6

Attachment

The third important structure of the self is that of "attachment". From the early childhood human beings enter into the relationship of attachment to all kinds of things – to things, people and ideas. At the centre of the network of life, there lies our attachment to the family and friends dear to us, and to our personal possessions in the form of wealth, fame and position. We get attached to these things emotionally which takes hold of our lives in a strong way by controlling our motives and attitudes in such a way so that we feel compelled to satisfy our attachments at any cost. In any case, satisfying our attachments remains a matter of priority in our lives in all our actions. So the understanding of our attachments, their structure and the true nature is the most important dimension of self-knowledge.

The class of attachments which we called "attachment to ideas" is not a small matter, as it has a kind of 'blind' force to it. In the present climate we see very clearly how life has become totally corrupt under the influence of this blind force. We see how people are willing to lay down their lives for the sake of political or religious ideologies to which they are attached. Throughout their upbringing people are brainwashed or conditioned into beliefs which are sheer illusions and unscientific. But the credulous are carried away by it and sacrifice their lives in vain for illusions.

Attachment is the greatest danger to life, because it breeds fear, anxiety and all other negative emotions connected with it. And there is great dissipation in it simply because it gives a tremendous sense of security. But it is a false sense of security.

If the whole structure of attachments is put aside, one will notice that there is no 'I'. The ego has disappeared. The ego is just the bundle of attachments. Living with ego-centred consciousness is the greatest danger to a sane and natural life of freedom. Because attachments create a kind of prison, and we live inside this prison thinking that we are secure and happy. When we act from our attachment our actions are guided by the conditioned attitudes and emotions. We receive this conditioning all the time. In fact, we grow into it and think that there is nothing outside it. It has the feeling of 'truth' but in fact it is falsehood. The prison not only limits the field of our action but also gives us the illusion that there is nothing outside it.

In attachment we experience great sorrow when some big personal failure takes place. It is a danger to life all along our living it, because we are not able to see the extraordinary openness of the possibilities of life, the quality of its spontaneity and its creativity. Living by and for attachments is a total distortion of life. We limit the scope of life by our own choice.

Seeing this dangerous nature of attachment is most important perception for spiritual upliftment. When the human spirit sees its danger it exercises its capacity to drop it instantaneously, requiring no effort of will. The perception of the true nature of attachment serves as its own action of freedom from it.

In fact to allow this forest of attachment to grow around you is downright stupidity. You are going to be lost in this forest. And you are going to lose your most natural endowments of potentialities. One such endowment is the human capacity to 'stand back' and look at a problem situation as a whole, and also completely afresh. The latter capacity requires that you are not carrying the baggage of the past, which all of us are. Our conditioning in the social, psychological and the physical environment is so subtle and so constant that we turn almost into 'mechanical' beings.

Attachment as the Provider of Security

This matter of attachment's connection with seeking security has to be understood very clearly, since security seems to be a fundamental demand of the conditioned mind. It has two sides. First, there is 'physical' insecurity. Our biological make-up is such that from birth the infant needs food etc. The body is not self-sufficient. It is dependent on external environmental resources. Here the mother fixes the central role of the provider. The infant gets attached to the mother and without her feels insecure. Similarly, the grown-up adults add security. They have to provide for themselves and their families, food, shelter and other daily necessities for survival. A child must feel secure at school to attend to his studies. And the teacher must feel secure to attend to his duties of teaching etc. In most civilised societies now-a-days, the physical security is not hard to get. But that is not where our main problem lies.

It is in the realm of the 'inner', the psychological that all human beings feel terribly insecure. Man is insecure in his very being, in his own consciousness of his self. The self-image with which he identifies himself is built upon his relationships with people or with ideas or with things. In case of people, all his relationships are constantly changing. They are not permanent in content and meaning. If you are a father, your children are growing up and acquiring a personality of their own. Your wife is a person, an independent ego, in her own right, and similarly with other people. The relationship between egos is perpetually disturbed, and implicitly at least, it is always in conflict. So we turn to relatively more permanent things like religion and nation or ideals of self-sacrifice, patriotism etc. But these are not real entities, they are man-made, conceptual constructs. So our relationship with them can never impart a sense of permanence to our being. One's being as "I-this, I-that" is itself in constant motion. I never invoke my identity as a child, it is being forgotten. My present identity consults only a limited number of relevant facts of my present situation. We hardly realise that our identity is constructed by thought, selected by memory and enriched by successes in achievements. All of which carry no constancy.

Nevertheless, we are terribly attached to our self-identity, which is a residue of our attachment with various people, things and ideals. And through these attachments we seek security on the psychological level. The bonds of attachment give you a sense of permanence, a sense of support for stability in your being. But if the above considerations are valid, it is clear that they only succeed in creating an illusion of security. In real life there is no such thing as psychological security.

Attachments are most compelling source of illusions. They invariably lead us to misinterpret our relationship. If, for example, I am attached to my wife, the attachment may lead me to a strong conviction that she loves me. Similar may be the case on her side, while the fact is neither. But one day when the fact confronts us in a crisis situation, we are not ready to deal with it. We break down and life becomes miserable. So if we are aware of attachments and the illusions they are creating, in an understanding mode, without hiding or running away from them, then we see the danger of living in illusions. And when one sees something fundamentally dangerous to one's living, it is a law of nature that one does not cling to it.

Attachment as the Source of Suffering

In life almost anything can become a source of suffering. We are thinking here of the psychological state of mind which we call suffering. Suffering whose source is in physical ailments are controllable from the outside. But suffering whose source is psychological is difficult to eliminate. It can drive people to madness or neurotic behaviour with varying degrees of aggressiveness. At any rate, it makes it very difficult to live a sane life.

Now, the main source of psychological suffering lies in our attachments. Attachment means 'clinging to' or 'holding on to' or simply 'not shaking off' what one is attached to. We are attached to all kinds of things – to property, to children and family and to our position or social status. But we get attached to anything which is continued source of pleasure. Sex, food, comfort and admiration are most common things in this category. But subtly and more dangerously, attachment to 'ideas' is great source of suffering. We are brought up and conditioned into religious beliefs, into beliefs of patriotism and beliefs of greatness of self-sacrifice for some 'cause' etc. But when any of these beliefs and attachments already mentioned are threatened (which is inevitable), we feel so frustrated and angry that we go to the extent of violence to meet the threat. And this sort of situation is a great source of suffering to oneself and a cause of suffering to others. The emotions involved in this situation always use up wastefully tremendous amount of psychic energy. Inwardly one is drained out, pitiable and miserable. And all this is due to one's attachment to the cause for which he is sacrificing himself. Attachment is always self-destructive. And there is the love of an idea – the pleasure and the sense of security, for example, that we derive in belief in reincarnation etc. And when that pleasure is denied, the frustration it produces can easily turn into hatred and violence. But is there love which is not pleasure-based, which is not trampled by desire, which is not mutilated by war of egos in personal relationship between two people? Is there love which blossoms in one's heart and whose fragrance can be enjoyed by anyone who comes near you. Such love does not depend upon anyone else's response. Such love, as Krishnamurti puts it, has "the enormous feeling of compassion – compassion for everything, for everybody. Compassion for nature, compassion for the earth on which we live, so that we don't destroy the earth, the animals, the whole thing..." (Truth and Activity, P 134). Such lose which is unattached to anything in particular, which, as the Bible puts it "seeketh not its own". So attachment is not love. Attachment at its core is dependency, it is insufficiency. So it is always insecure. It always has underpinning of fear and anxiety. By contrast love is non-attachment, it has no motive. It is fearless and intrepid in choosing life in freedom and creativity. It is freedom from the past. So that the new can emerge. It is creativity at the highest level of your being.

However, non-attachment is not something which can be consciously practised. It is not "detachment", something which can be attained by suppression of desires, by rejection of objects of attachment, by imposition of will. Will itself is an implication of attachment, of desire. Non-attachment is something which has to 'happen' to an individual. The Upanishads maintain that it can arise only in total understanding of the nature and structure of the self. Buddha taught the same thing. But the theistic strand of Hinduism maintains that it can arise only in total surrender to God, in the spontaneity of the love of the divine. But it has to be remembered that surrender itself is not an 'act of will'. One cannot decide and choose to surrender. We know adverse physical changes take place in the state of high emotion. Normality is lost, some people even suffer heart attack or stroke or hidden diseases like ulser etc. In fact, highly charged 'pleasurable' emotions are also self-destructive. It is common knowledge that a sudden news of some great unexpected gain can cause heart attack as much as news of great sorrow. In both cases the emotion's connection with the degree of attachment is the culprit.

Why does this happen? The answer is that to a large extent we 'are' our attachments. Attachment defines our inner psychological identity or who we are psychologically. The self is a bundle of attachments. As long as this belief is there, sorrow is inevitable.

But sorrow is not their only when some big adverse event happens. Sorrow is embedded in the daily life of everyone, rich or poor, weak or strong. It is embedded in the daily travail, going to work against one's wishes to earn a living, struggling to become this or that position-holder, struggling to maintain harmony in personal relationship, struggling to avoid conflicts. But conflict is inevitable when your ego is dealing with another ego. You may make adjustment for the sake of superficial peace. But there is so much pain in living a life which is full of constant adjustments.

We have seen how becoming is another source of sorrow. Our whole life is constantly seeking to become – rich, famous, powerful with prestige and status. But the direction of becoming stems from attachment – attachment to one's self-image. Generally we hold on to our self-image, which we have ourselves created, all our lives, we do not know what our real self is, we do not understand either its nature or structure or its operational motivations. All that we know is our self-image, which drives us to attain, to achieve more and more. We have the idea that the more we possess the happier we will be. But are we? We never question this. To "possess" is psychologically a factor of attachment. It breeds anxiety about protecting our possessions. And in the process of living we miss on the joy of harmonious loving relationship. Relationships become burdened with fear, greed, violence and sorrow. All these inner psychological burdens stem from various attachments.

The sages naturally saw the causes of suffering in the larger, necessary and universal features of life. Buddha, for example, saw suffering embedded in the natural processes of growth and decay of life. Change with the passage of time, disease, old age and death are all imbued with sorrow and suffering. Then there is the all-prevailing fear of the unknown, of 'tomorrow'. True, man has many theories about them to console him but the fear continues suppressed and curled up in the heart of existence.

Fear and anxiety govern all walks of life. The threatening uncertainty and the ephemeral character of life remain a constant challenge for man, forcing him into unremitting struggle and conflict. So we develop attachments and cling to them. Man is condemned to live by the memories of the past.

In attachment there is always a hidden struggle between hope and fear. One is attached to beliefs, to the authority of gurus, to faiths and their corresponding personalities. One is constantly reinforcing one's convictions, suppressing doubts, suppressing anti-emotions, etc. But there is always lurking in the background a frightful uncertainty. In the heart of hearts you know that you don't know. You hope but you are really not sure. This unconscious struggle dissipates your energy – the energy which you need to find out the truth for yourself, the energy which you need in daily life for a sane and creative living. So attachment is a great source of self-destruction. It gives you a sense of security, no doubt. But to maintain that sense of security itself needs a great deal of energy. Because, again, in the depth of our hearts we know that there is no such thing as security. Our lives are constantly changing, the whole universe is constantly changing, and any moment any little change can acquire a huge significance for the whole of life. So the sense of security is illusory. It is the greatest illusion in life and we tend to erect the vast edifice of our lives upon this illusion. So no matter how we look at it, we find that attachment is not only the main source of suffering, it is a 'silent killer' in day-to-day life as well.

Unfortunately, many will object to my valuation of attachment. In modern liberal civilisation people tend to attach great personal value to their personal affections. And that is carried over to the attachments we develop in this connection. Attachment to family and friends in personal affectionate relationships measures the degree of your caring for that relationship. In fact, it is taken as a measure of your love for that person. But if we look at this phenomenon carefully we find that attachment bears none of the qualities which the profound and most sacred quality of love carries with it. In what has come to be called 'love', first of the extent of our attachments is enormous. From the early infancy and the experience of breast feed, we are conditioned into various dependencies. In our relationship we grow into expecting various forms of fulfilments. Any frustration of our expectations turns into an experience of hurt. Wherever there are expectations there is bound to be hurt-feeling some or other time, for the other has his own expectations. The other does not exist simply to fulfil your expectations. So wherever there is even a small amount of fulfilment, there is a tendency to get attached to it.

It seems that bonds of attachment confer a sense of permanence to all the relationships, and by implication, they keep our hope of fulfilment in future alive. In 'permanence' there is a strange sense of security as well. Psychologically, we seem to need this sense of security in 'permanence', even though we know it to be illusory. We know, as the Buddha taught, that in reality nothing is permanent. We see all the relationships changing their character with time. Children, for example, grow up and your wife gets older and the whole mood of your relationship with them is transformed. Everyone is familiar with the all powerful factor of change in the temporal world, but psychologically no one wants to accept it. The reason is obvious. No one wants to end his expectations of fulfilments. So one creates an illusion of 'permanence' through the bonds of attachment.

There is, however, another deeper reason for this. Subliminally, we are all aware of a bottomless emptiness within ourselves. When we look within, we cannot find any attribute with which we can identify ourselves. Yet we firmly believe that we are substantially the same entities all our lives. The thought of not finding a substantial and permanent "self" is unbearable. So we turn to our bundle of attachments which gives a sense of a unique identity. But the substantiality, uniqueness and permanence attached to one's individual self remain a roller-coaster of illusions.

Now, since our attachments are the source of our personal motives, it is clear that if we could eliminate them from our psyche, and respond directly to life, we would be living a life of non-attachment. To be able to do that would mean that inwardly one is not living for oneself. It would mean that one's relationship with one's works has changed. Will it be worth it? Will not a life of non-attachment be simply a mechanical affair? I think from what we have said so far the answer is definitely "no". The answer is that when one has eliminated personal motives of becoming, which emanate from attachments, one would be living a life simply for "the love of life". And love, as noted earlier, is exactly that "which seeketh not its own". When one's relationship with one's works is love, one is living like as "Artist of Life". Love is creativity in whatever one does without the motive of self-promotion. As we saw, when a musician creates his music for the love of it, he is not bothered about what money or fame he is going to get from it. Then his work of creativity is not simply a means to further ends of personal advantage. His work is an end in itself and he is one with it.

This kind of creative living in non-attachment, however, is not an exclusive domain of talented people. Rather, whatever one does in freedom from personal motives, flows from the spiritual background of "selflessness" and has that 'extra' quality of creativity.

Non-attachment

By contrast, a life of freedom from attachments would mean "living for the love of life". In this a man is not pushed into relationship by the blind impulsive forces of attachment. His life is not governed by the grasping aspect of the "me". Without attachments, the grip of fear and becoming upon life is weakened and the overall character of his life is transformed from self-centred motives to the inspirations of love and compassion. The conditioned framework of "desire-anger-possessiveness-greed" which normally guides all his choices is put aside and he is ushered into a new era of creativity, spontaneity and freedom. In creative living there is unimpeded manifestation of his talents and intelligence. His activities are not censored by the motives of security and fulfilment of the self.

Love is not attachment. As we have seen, attachment moves from the motive of insecurity. But surely, when the motive behind an act is one's emotional security, it can't be truly described as "love". As the Bible says, "Love is that which seeketh not its own". Love is always in the present. It has no personal future or the past. The vitality, the strength and the beauty of love lie in its intrinsic character of "non-attachment".

The overall effect of being in non-attachment is a transformed life of love and creativity. In attachment mode we always relate to life with the desire of acquiring something. That is, we look at the world with the eyes of "what is in it for me". Our concern with the world is always self-centred, demanding pleasure and security. So we relate to life always with the violence of possessiveness, the arrogance of greed and the aggressiveness of becoming. But with the bonds of attachment broken we can now relate to the world with love and compassion and the joy of moment to moment creativity.

The works done in non-attachment are most significantly connected with the final goal of liberation. Such works 'do not build one' to the world. Because, as the Gita says, in such works one is inwardly "disinterested" or "udaseen". 'Disinterestedness' here does not mean "uninterested". What it means is that even the greatest of works is done without a sense of pride or personal glory or achievement. One does what one does without emphasising one's own role as the architect of success, that is, without the ego attached to it. In 'disinterestedness' and non-attachment one is 'unambitious' about one's own works and inwardly one is 'indifferent' to the nature of the results that accrue upon them. In this state of mind one is aware of the ugliness or the beauty of one's works without either wanting or denying it, without either accepting or rejecting it. In this state, one is completely sensitive to everything around one and does one's best in what one has undertaken to do.

Normally one works with two kinds of motives behind one's actions. One is the straightforward motive of success in the technical sense, and the other is, inwardly a personal motive of success in the psychological dimension. It is the latter kind of motive which has no place in actions from non-attachment.

Finally, the virtue of non-attachment is seen to stand out in the field of ethical actions. Especially, in resolving moral dilemmas, where standard moral theories breakdown, non-attachment helps the moral agent in taking a holistic view of the dilemma and thus arrive at the correct resolution. A classic case of such a dilemma is discussed between Arjuna and Krishna in the battle field of Kurukshetra. Let us see how Krishna's holistic considerations help Arjuna get out of his moral predicament.

Arjuna has obviously arrived at the battlefield with every intention of fighting after having duly considered the situation in consultation with others concerned. His reasons for fighting are connected with a moral theory which gets its meaning from the notion of an ideal society (ramrajya) in which the principle of justice must be upheld at all costs. Arjuna has characterised the opponents as unjust and criminal. He sees that they are filled with greed, and have geared themselves to this horrible war for the sake of their personal gratification. Thus, Arjuna is in no doubt about the unworthiness of the Kauravas' ambitions and the legitimacy of his own right to kill them. Yet a doubt has crept into his mind. Is it really worth it? Standing on the battlefield face to face with his opponents it has suddenly dawned upon him (though he must have already known it) that the battle involves killing his own kinsmen, his affectionate friends, his respected elders, and revered gurus. His initial response is highly emotional. 'I do not wish to kill them, even for the gain of the kingdom of all the three worlds'. But later he reasons from the point of view of self-interest. He says that he does not envisage any personal happiness at regaining the kingdom when all his near and dear ones have been killed. One cannot enjoy any gain at such a cost. 'Having slained my own kinsmen and so on, what shall I do with the kingdom and the pleasures of life?' But there is much more to Arjuna's reasoning. There now follows a whole lot of solid moral reasons for the shift in his attitude. These reasons seem to be connected with a different moral theory from the one suggested in favour of his earlier decision to fight. It is a theory which gets its meaning and purpose from a social context which was very real in Arjuna's cultural milieu. The traditional obligations which he now invokes are embedded in a way of life in which the loyalty to one's clan, the happiness of one's kinsmen and friends, and respect for one's elders and gurus seems to be considered the most important. Thus, notwithstanding the legitimacy of his right to kill the Kauravas, Ariuna argues on moral grounds that a family fight, since it leads to disastrous consequences for the whole clan, must be avoided. The battle is definitely going to destroy the clan, and such a battle is evidently evil. And the killing of friends and elders is clearly sinful. Moreover, Arjuna who, unlike the Kauravas, sees the bizarre future consequences of the war has a further reason for avoiding the fight. He makes the point that, while the Kauravas' have a limited vision of the war and ignore the horrors to come, 'we who understand the evils of such a war must try to avoid it'? Arjuna then goes on in some detail to trace the sequence of the consequences of the war in question as follows.

In the death of the elders and the gurus of the clan the structure of authority in the clan is destroyed. Then there fellows the decline of moral order in the clan. From this decline comes the corruption of the women of the family. This, in turn, leads to racial/caste intermixture and impurity in the whole clan, which leads them all to hell. And, further, since they are no longer offering "pind" to the deceased ancestors, they also suffer a fall in their spiritual status and perhaps remain in limbo. And, further, the numerous evils generated by racial caste impurity lead to the destruction of the established caste morality as well as clan morality, that is, of the moral order in society as a whole. The decline of moral order in society brings ruin and unhappiness to all, sending all of them finally to hell.

Krishna's Response

Keeping the above-mentioned complexity of moral obligation in mind; let us see how Krishna attempts to resolve the dilemma in question. His initial response in order to satisfy Arjuna on all the three counts, namely, emotional, prudential and ethical, appears to provide an odd mixture of moral and non-moral reasons. But, as his discourse develops, its moral character begins to dominate. Converting a mere family fight (in Arjuna's conception) into a dharmayuddha, Krishna considers Arjuna's conflict basically as a moral dilemma.

On the emotional front, Krishna admonishes Arjuna for his weakness of the will. He characterises Arjuna's state of mind as of 'moha', i.e. sentimental attachment. Such a state of mind deprives one of heavenly happiness and bestows notoriety upon one. Krishna condemns Arjuna for harbouring unmanly emotion which blinds one to one's own interests, weakens one for action, and blurs one's discriminative abilities making him like a dead man. Krishna spends a long time preaching that it is irrational to lament for the death of the body. The message is brought home finally by invoking the esoteric doctrines of the immortality of the soul and rebirth. The essential being of a person, the soul, is declared indestructible. After each death it is reborn. It casts away bodies like a man who discards old clothes and gets new ones. It is unworthy to feel attachment for the body, when the soul that 'wears' it is everlasting. A wise man does not identify himself with his body.

Next, Krishna argues that to allow oneself to be swayed by the emotion of grief and feel crippled by moha is clearly imprudent, for the inaction it recommends will bring one countless personal losses. He tells Arjuna that if he does not fight:

(a) People will call him a coward and he will lose honour and respect in the eyes of others;
(b) By failing to do what he is capable of as a warrior he will be losing the pleasures of life now and also the heavenly abode of the after life;
(c) On the other hand, if he is killed in this war, he will definitely go to heaven, and, if he wins, he will inherit the earth.

Having pointed out all these rewards for fighting, Krishna now quietly shifts his reasoning to the spiritual plane. He observes that the wise man remains calm through the drama of pleasures and pains. He does not lament a personal loss, nor rejoice in the gains; for both of these are irrelevant to the blissful being of the eternal self.

In his specifically moral reasoning Krishna declares the war to be a dharmayuddha, i.e. a righteous or just war. While Arjuna, though in doubt about the injustice done to him, had come to fight with the motive of personal gain of the kingdom, Krishna makes it clear that for a man in his position it was a moral obligation to fight. Such a war, far from being a sin, is the gateway to heaven. Rather, not fighting, i.e. not fulfilling his obligation, will involve him in sin and responsibility for all its terrible consequences. Moreover, there is nothing distinctively moral in acting with the motive of personal gain. Since one has right only to action and not to its 'fruits', one ought to act in non-attachment to the consequences of one's actions.

Thus, the overall character of Krishna's argument is clearly ethical. Its force is to the effect that a righteous war must be fought independently of considerations of personal gain or loss. This war is righteous, since it aims at justice which is the very foundation of human existence. Arjuna in his status as a warrior-prince has an obligation to fight.

If, in a given situation, two different sets of reasons, both prima facie equally good, dictate two different obligations, and it is not possible to enact both, nor to eliminate one by reference to a higher-order principle, and yet in actual life one has to choose one, then it is clear that one has to suppress one's propensity to realise one in favour of the other quite arbitrarily. And, for this reason, one is likely to feel remorse. In such cases, as Williams rightly suggests, moral conflicts are like conflicts of desire. And, further, he says, just as suppressing one desire in favour of the other one does not remove the former, by ignoring one moral obligation for the sake of fulfilling the other one has not really resolved the conflict. One has simply gone ahead despite the conflict. Thus, unlike conflicts of belief, in moral conflicts a moral 'remainder' remains uneliminable and is shown by the fact that one feels remorse for not being able to carry out the ignored 'ought'. Now, Arjuna's conflict turns out to illustrate this point clearly. For, as Krishna suspects, Arjuna's primary motive in contemplating surrender is to give vent to his sentiments, and the cause of this lies in his attachments. True, Arjuna gives solid moral reasons in support of his revised attitude. But then, earlier, he had equally good reasons for contemplating killing the very same people whom he now thinks he cannot and should not kill. In adopting this new attitude, he has simply suppressed his earlier decision. But, as we have said, abandoning one horn of the dilemma in favour of the other does not dissolve the conflict. What, one might ask, justifies Arjuna's shift in his attitude? For simply stating a new set of reasons implying a contrary obligation does not show that his earlier reasons were morally inferior. And Arjuna has done nothing to prove that they are. He has simply given new reasons to support his revised attitude. Indeed, his new attitude is dictated by his sentiments and attachments. And the fact that he adduces new reasons to justify his new attitude towards the war is secondary, and is itself determined by his sentiments. His reasons may be good, but the ground for drawing upon a new set of reasons instead of sticking to the earlier ones is itself arational; it is rooted in his affections and fears. That is, his moral dilemma springs not simply from a conflict between two different sets of reasons, both valid in the situation, but also from an inheritance of conflicting values and their accompanying sentiments in his psyche.

In general, our sentiments and fears cannot be divorced from what we value and the reasons we, in fact, give to support our practical decisions. A dilemma-situation is only a special case of a situation in which one has to decide between different alternatives. For the same situation could, in principle, depending upon our sentiments, desires and dispositions, elicit different interpretations and consequently set in motion different chains of reasons yielding different 'oughts'. And if the conflicting 'oughts' cannot be brought under one overriding principle, then we have a moral dilemma. So, given that there is no one absolute, objective and integrated set of ultimate moral principles, reason alone cannot resolve a moral dilemma. In the case of a complex moral conflict as deep as that of Arjuna's, in which a whole way of life is challenged, the wayout is not simply to abandon one 'ought' and opt for the other on the strength of one's present intuitive appreciation of the depth of the reasons supporting them. For, as we have seen, the strength of one's present conviction alone does not prove that the earlier conviction was morally inferior. Rather, an arbitrary choice will be considered degenerate in a way in which his present state is not, since, although conflicting, it is at least rooted in his own experience of life, and, therefore, expresses his real choices. For an authentic resolution of the conflict, it is necessary that one does not simply ignore one part of the conflict, but that it be purged out of one's psyche from its very roots. And, further, the alternative which is expelled is actually apprehended as morally inferior or in some sense illusory. And, again, if the choice has been made by reference to a new discovery of an ultimate principle, then the discovery must be of the nature of a radical conversion, a total transformation of one's outlook on life. And the new outlook must be self-evidently morally superior.

What is most interesting and important in Krishna's approach to the resolution of the conflict is precisely this: that finally Krishna is able to affect the relevant kind of radical conversion or enlightenment. From what we have said so far, it is clear that Krishna's response to Arjuna on the three counts, namely, emotional, prudential and ethical, has more or less had the effect of simply underlining, in a more articulate way, Arjuna's earlier judgments and attitudes. By providing Arjuna with good reasons for sticking to his earlier decision, Krishna has not really resolved his dilemma. His task is still incomplete. For, although he has correctly identified the cause of Arjuna's dejection and the motive behind the shift in his attitude, he has not shown that Arjuna's new stand is morally unjustified.

Krishna now realises that to get Arjuna out of the dilemma he has to make him look at the situation in a completely new way. Both Arjuna's judgments, the earlier and the revised, regarding the desirability of the battle are made within a frame of reference which reflects an incomplete picture of reality. The picture is not radically incoherent, rather it contains blemishes that are corrigible. Arjuna's conflicting interpretation of the situation shows his ignorance of the underlying reality which supports it. Krishna seems to believe that, if only Arjuna could see the imminent battle in the context of the whole of cosmic reality, he would emerge from his confused state of mind and take the right decision. For this reason, Krishna enlarges the scope of his discourse to cover the area of transcendental knowledge. He explains the underlying unity of cosmic reality, including the nature of such things as the self, death and the creation of cosmic beings, matter and mind, action and predestination, etc. The casuistic resources of his discourse tends to correct Arjuna's ontological worldview. But, while the discourse may have altered many of Arjuna's beliefs about the situation he was in, it was not sufficient to change his sentiments and fears which, we have seen, were the basic determinants of the shift in his reasoning. No doubt beliefs do limit the range of one's desires, and make one consider some fears as baseless and some sentiments as unnecessary. But beliefs by themselves cannot eliminate these, and transform one's total sense of values. In order to affect that transformation, one needs the impact of first-hand experience and knowledge of the highest kind. Thus, in the present ease, the relevant experience cannot be of any ordinary kind, but somewhat different, although nevertheless within the empirical framework of mundane life; for the conflicting axiological frame of reference of Arjuna's dilemma is already a residue of the richness and the variety of his experience of life. It is because Arjuna is an 'insider' vis-à-vis this frame of thought that he is a victim of the dilemma in the first place. For him to be able to perceive his situation as a whole he has to step outside the present experiential framework. And this is precisely what is made available to Arjuna in a vision of cosmic reality. In this Arjuna perceives the entire process of cosmic creation and destruction. He sees how individual souls are involved in the order of nature and what it would mean to attain spiritual freedom. He sees the true nature of thought, action, emotion, etc. Seeing all this, his attachment to mortal existence is destroyed, and the sentiments and fears consequent upon his attachment disappear. He is free from moha, and relinquishing all thoughts of personal gain he is now in a position to act from the motive of duty alone.

How exactly the perception of the 'whole', the vision affects this transformation in Arjuna is not easy to understand. There is obviously no strictly logical step from what one experiences to what one values and desires. Nevertheless, it is not impossible to guess what may have happened. Since the vision is a totally new experience, it must produce structural changes in the subject's psyche, resulting in a significantly new orientation of the mind. So, realising not only intellectually but deeply, existentially, that the inner self is immortal, Arjuna now feels no grief at the thought of the death of his affectionate and respected ones. Similarly, seeing that the war is inevitable and that he is only instrumental to it, Arjuna no longer fears killing his elders. And, realising that in acting without the motive of personal gain one stands outside the order of causes and effects, he no longer fears that he will be infected by sin in killing the elders, etc. The result of this new orientation of mind is that certain considerations drop out as irrelevant in determining how to act. Thus, for example, the fact that Arjuna's dear ones will die in the war becomes irrelevant to the question of fighting a righteous war. Similarly, in the light of the revelation of the true nature of the self and its implication in the order of causes, the fact that the immediate consequences of the war will be hellish appears insignificant. And, further, Arjuna's earlier emotions and the reasons they suggested are rendered irrelevant.

It is, therefore, not unreasonable to assume that, from the vantage point of truth, the enlightened man's mind will embrace only one set of values, and that one set of values must be internally coherent, and must somehow reflect the true and eternal order in nature. Since it is impossible for the natural intelligence of man to believe that reality is internally incoherent, it is impossible for reason to accept that the same reality, when lived and directly experienced, will imprint upon the enlightened mind a set of conflicting values and sentiments.

The principle that the perception of truth alone is sufficient to bring about a total transformation of the human psyche has been upheld in all the major branches of Indian spiritual philosophy. Furthermore, the enlightened being is characterised as a 'free' being. In the state of spiritual freedom, the mind of the individual is identical with the mind of God, or, what amounts to the same thing, the individual merges into the Divine; and, therefore, in his actions, he is no longer guided by the limitations of his individual ego. It is, therefore, not difficult to see that an enlightened man must be free from all conflicts of beliefs as well as of emotions, and would naturally will one thing. Then there would be no room for a moral dilemma. Further, it is needless to defend the moral superiority of the decisions taken in the state of spiritual freedom. On the attainment of enlightenment, involving total understanding of human existence, man has reached the culmination of his spiritual evolution. When a man acts from the standpoint of truth, how could his action not be morally supreme?

We are now in a position to make the following comment on Krishna's ethical standpoint. He does vindicate an ethical monism, but a qualified one. It is suggested that, so long as our knowledge is limited to the empirical world, we are not in a position to grasp the ultimate ethical significance of a given situation and the choices we make in it. From our limited point of view, neither intuition nor reason nor the principle of utility can ensure that no genuine moral dilemmas will arise. But when our knowledge is extended to the eternal order of causes, and one understands the fundamental structures of human existence, then, from that vision of truth, one is in no doubt as to which action is morally supreme. The understanding works on our reason through the resolution of conflicts in our emotions. Virtue is necessary to moral choice, and non-attachment is necessary to virtue.

7

Enlightenment and Freedom

The overall character of enlightenment is episodic – a sudden dissolution of all the major illusions of life connected with the human condition. At the centre of these lies the grand illusion of the substantiality and the individuality of a separate self for each human being. The "I", the self, takes its solid personal existence for granted. Without knowing 'who' or 'what' it is, it pursues its existence relentlessly. It is manifest in the consciousness that one is separate individual self, and the desire to remain implicated in the pursuit of its continuous existence. We have seen that this "desire to be" sees no option but to pursue existence through "becoming". This blind pursuit of existence through personal achievements, imbued with conflicts and the consequent sorrow, is continued passionately till death. One never questions its origin and its reality. One is born in ignorance of its truth and dies in ignorance. Of course, one lives with various belief systems about its nature and destiny, but belief is not equivalent to knowledge. And knowledge, in case of something like the self and personal existence, can never be simply conceptual or 'by description' alone. It has to be 'experiential'. Consciousness is not a descriptive concept; it has no phenomenological properties and it is not computational. One knows it only in being conscious. But we have acquired and live by the concept of the self. The consciousness of the "separateness" of the individual self is, as we have seen, built into the nature of thought – it is conceptual not primeval, original or before thought.

So, the central episodic event of enlightenment, must if it is to deliver truth, consist in a return to pre-thought consciousness and perception in a flash as it were, of the origin of the individual self – its separation from being and the nature of its operational existence in time. Enlightenment, thus, is meant to be nothing short of an experiential knowledge or a direct perception of truth itself – that is the 'whole' consisting of the order of "being-consciousness, the individual and the world". If enlightenment is an insight into the order of existence as a whole, it must be a knowing not by thought but by being it, and having self-intuition in being it. If one wonders why thought is so important in knowing the 'order of existence' as a whole, one has simply to look inwardly and recognise the fact that thought itself is one movement within the vastness of consciousness and therefore represents only a fraction of its being. Thought cannot come out of being, as it were, and look at it as an observer.

Normally, as we have noted, knowing requires a separation of the object known from the knower, but 'knowing by being' to be possible, the knower itself must be by its own nature, of the form of a "knowing-being". Consciousness, as we have seen, is of this form – to be conscious is necessarily to know simultaneously that one is thus and so. When consciousness as a whole is aware of the total order of existence, it will also be simultaneously aware of its being thus and so, that is, of its being as a totality and completeness. Naturally this complete awareness of itself will include awareness of the constitution of the world and the individual selves. In the enlightened individual this signifies a state of total 'wakefulness', like the one which, for instance, Buddha attributed to himself when asked about how different he felt after enlightenment. It is the original and timeless state of consciousness per se which is absorbed in absolute creativity and is simultaneously aware of it. Surely, in the act of highest creativity, though consciousness is 'absorbed' in the act, it must also be subliminally as it were, aware of its creativity, to experience that extraordinary joy that accompanies it. It is in this latter role of 'simultaneous awareness' of its creativity, that consciousness can be seen as the highest self or God. Enlightenment, therefore, is a participation in God-consciousness by the individual. There is no other to behold him, none to comprehend him, there is no knowledge of him, except by him within himself. (Matsya Purana).

The best theoretical account of the content of enlightened state in the individual can be abstracted from the non-dualistic interpretation of Vedanta given by Shankara. I will now attempt a brief exposition of it in modern terminology.

In Shankara's account the whole content of enlightenment can be summed up in three truths which he expresses in one verse:

> That is, "Brahma satyam, jagan mithya, jivo Brahmaiv na parah"
> Brahman is, the world is not, the individual and Brahman are not distinct.

"Brahman" is usually translated as existence or reality or truth or power or energy which creates, sustains, destroys and recreates the very substance of the universe. Shankara identifies three characteristics of Brahman which are being, consciousness and bliss. These three are interconnected manifestations of "one divine reality" of the Rigveda which is Brahman. In thinking of reality as a whole, it is important to think of all the three in an inclusive fashion. For, being without "knowing" that it is being is reduced to nothingness – an inert in itselfness".

This function of knowing is performed by consciousness. Consciousness alone knows that it is and thus attaining the status of being. The third constituent in bliss or joy. It represents the aesthetic dimension of existence. And Shankara, rightly again, in thinking of reality as a whole, thinks of bliss as an inalienable but distinct strand of Brahman. For manpower and consciousness without joy can't be an "end-in-itself" which the concept of divinity requires. Power and consciousness can be "means" of existence but can't provide "purpose" which intelligence of the universe requires to move to an end which represents a fulfilment in itself. The concept of God represents all this – of power, creativity and of being an end in himself.

It is to the greatness of Shankara's thought that he has hit upon the ultimate nature of reality in a most general and inclusive concept. How does one know that it is correct? It seems to require the following two standards: (1) Any answer must be ultimately "intelligible" in terms of non-technical concepts that we have. (2) The answer must be in terms of "inalienable features" of human experience. And it seems to me that the answer given by Shankara stands to these requirements. We have more to say about it shortly.

The second truth is the world is not or "is unreal" i.e. "mithya". The following points can be made in support of this view:

1. The evanescence of time lends itself to a sense of the unreality of the world. With the consciousness of the passage of time, even in an ordinary contemplation of the second truth, the "not-ness" or "nothingness" of the world dawns upon one with the force of a mystical experience. One feels that

the world melts away in the flow of time. And time itself exists only in memory. And time-past and time-future can both be held only in the slippery hold of the present. The sense of Shankara's claim that the world is "mithya" becomes vividly glaring. Past has vanished, the future is not there yet and the present is real only if it is forced by the mind to be speciously stationery. The world is swallowed up by time which itself melts away into nothingness if not remembered. In this way the world is unreal in the sense of being "insubstantial" or simply existing as a 'phenomenon' without the backing of any tangible substance.

2. The second point is that the world Shankara is concerned with, the "Sansara", is not the hard reality of the senses, but the world created in the intentional nexus. Shankara is keen to reflect on the religious significance of the world in which we are caught up in pursuing ends and goals – the intentional world of achievements. It is the world of relationships with objects, with people and other creatures. This world exists only in our desiring fulfilment through personal achievements. The point is that the goals we pursue have no intrinsic worth and they are supplied by the social environment in which one is placed at the time one lives his life. In another time they would either not exist or will be considered worthless. Such a world is like a dream in which one can pursue one's desires to great extents of satisfaction.
3. The third point is that the lived-world or the perceived world is largely a conceptual construct. We do not see things as they are in themselves. Nor do we see the reality from which our perceived-world springs. Whatever may be going on behind the scene, this

much is certain that what we perceive, the 'finished product', as it were, is the result of our putting the 'raw materials' of the universe in the world of our concepts. The capacity to form concepts is an art, as Kant puts it, "hidden in the depths of the human soul". Moreover, from the sotereological point of view, it is clear that the world in which we give shape to our aspirations and ambitions, and the world in which we struggle to realise our ends and purposes, is a world which can't exist 'outside', as it were, of human inter-subjectivity. The existence of a purposive world 'in rerun', as it were simply has no meaning. The intelligible world pops up only in our relatedness as a conceptual construct for and by the 'players', i.e. the human subjects, who are capable of responding to the hidden reality with thought.

Liberation (Mukti, Moksha or Nirvana)

Liberation or spiritual freedom is the consequence of enlightenment. It signifies a state of consciousness in which the liberated individual loses his ego-centred awareness of the world, entering the world of absolute creativity of Brahman. The liberated soul acquires a participatory consciousness with Brahman. And in this sense he becomes one with Brahman. From the human point of view, what is important to realise is that the liberated soul lives and moves around in the world without the 'centre', the 'I' or the sense of being a separate individual consciousness, and consequently, without assigning any experiences to himself. From the objective point of view, for others, what he says or does, are naturally attributed to the individual person who is identified by reference to a particular body. But, for himself, inwardly, he is not an individual and does not claim to 'own' experiences which are his rather than others. There is a total shift in his point of view upon himself and others. As the Gita puts it:

Naturally, the liberated soul who has lost an individualistic point of view upon the world, has inwardly resolved all the conflicts that arise solely due to the division between "mine" and-not-mine". As a result he does not lament any loss, simply because he never incurs any personal loss, and he does not experience any sorrow which is always associated with some kind of personal loss.

The result of this shift of the point of view upon life is far-reaching. The important one to note is the fact that he has no urge any longer for "becoming" which, as we have seen, arises out of the fear of non-being. Now, when he sees "himself in everyone and everyone in himself", when he is one with Brahman, all "change" in the universe is an expression of his own creativity. In creativity, there is no separation between the creator and the creation. There is "being-in-becoming". It is a process of a moment to moment creativity, which can be looked upon both as 'being' and 'becoming' simultaneously. Time and space are internal to this creativity and the process itself is not in time and space.

Since the seeking and becoming has stopped, there is freedom "in" the individual, and not that the individual 'is free' to choose as he wishes. Of course, from the objective point of view, as his body is placed in varying situations, he will be making relevant choices, but inwardly he is not appropriating these choices for the sake of individual self-fulfilment.

The transcendental fallout of this freedom, in the context of the doctrine of rebirth, is that the individual self has broken the chain of transmigration. Since his desire for becoming is extinct, he has no need for rebirth. So this freedom can be described as "freedom from rebirth". But the expression "freedom from" carries a misleading suggestion which has to be avoided. It suggests that after enlightenment everything remains the same with the individual, except that he will not be reborn. That is, he may live for ever on the spiritual plane, in a splendid isolation of his soul from the natural world in which he will never be born again. But this suggestion ignores the logical truth that a pure spirit has no identity and cannot be treated as an 'individual', which has to be distinguished as one among many.

Nor, can the individual 'live for ever' in the sense that he carries the consciousness of his unity with Brahman and retains it "within" Brahman. For, in that case he will retain the consciousness of being an individual self also. And then logically speaking his consciousness of unity with Brahman will signify only an "external" relation with Brahman. It will not signify a consciousness of being an integral part of Brahman, of "internal" relation with Brahman, like a wave in the ocean, as described by Shankara in Advaita philosophy. But that is what is precisely required by "enlightenment" leading to freedom as we have understood above.

It might be thought that since the doctrine of rebirth is highly esoteric and limited to the religions of Indian origin, the Hindu idea of spiritual freedom will have no appeal for mankind in general. Then the focus of man's spiritual quest will shift to the notion of "good life", as it has been by and large in Western philosophy. The primary question for man would not be how to attain freedom from rebirth, but how to live this present and only life in the best possible way.

However, in the Hindu view these two points of view are not separated, because the belief in rebirth is not a presupposition of their quest but a discovery. The primary question both in ethics and metaphysics is "what is truth?" And that is reduced to the question: "What is the knower of truth?" The pursuit of self-knowledge, therefore, is at once an attempt to answer both: what is a good life? And what is the ultimate truth? Surely, it will be generally agreed that our settled goals and purposes have doubtful value if one is ignorant of the nature and destiny of the self for which the goals and purposes exist in the first place.

Spiritual freedom accrues upon enlightenment which consists of a total experiential knowledge of the supreme truth. So the Hindu prayer for enlightenment reads:

> Lead us from darkness to Light,
> Lead us from evil to the Good,
> Lead us from death to non-death.

This shows that 'freedom' is an inclusive concept. The state of spiritual freedom consists of the satisfaction of the whole prayer as above.

1. It is a state in which 'ignorance', 'evil' and 'death' are replaced by the light of the supreme knowledge of truth, goodness and transcendence of temporality.
2. It is a state in which all illusions are removed and so fear is allayed for ever.
3. It is a state in which all sorrow is annihilated and the individual human spirit suffering from its isolation in separation from being, returns to the universal spirit of God and experiences the eternal "unity of being" in God.
4. It is a state in which consciousness rejoins its 'purity'.

Purity of Consciousness

'Purity of consciousness' does not mean a consciousness

devoid of any experiential content. There can be no such consciousness. As we have said earlier, consciousness is always directed towards something which it holds as its "object" or left to itself, it always has some experiential content. But in pure consciousness experiences are "unowned" i.e. the contents are not claimed or followed along or accompanied by a self-consciousness. In its religious meaning we can say that a pure consciousness is not presided over by an ego. And, consequently, it is not accumulated as "one's experience" in personal memory. Experiences occur and pass away without creating a personal "past". Nor do they create a personal future. This is so because the being with pure consciousness does not hanker to possess what he has experienced. He has no desire to possess experienced or imagined objects for future satisfaction. And so he is always open to the newness of life. Pure consciousness is a timeless movement of freedom of the spirit.

The pure consciousness which does not desire to possess anything, physically or psychologically, naturally has no fear of their loss, or lamentation for not having owned them. He does not lament anything even the loss of good health, wealth or pleasurable objects. Naturally, again, he has no fear of death even, for death is nothing but the loss of family, wealth of life on earth.

Possessing consciousness in its purity signifies a return to pure subjectivity in which the individual regains his spiritual status as an eternal "subject" and never an "object" for himself. To be a subject is one thing and to possess the knowledge, consciousness that one is a subject is quite another thing. The knowledge, which as we have seen is a function of thought, gives isolation to the subject – the subject identifies itself with a limited number of experiences as its individual identity. By possessing knowledge of one's stream of consciousness, the pure subject self creates a secondary, empirically, self and forgets its true nature. This isolation into individuality is a condition of knowledge, which is reversed in the condition of freedom.

So freedom is indeed 'freedom-from'. It is freedom from sorrow, from fear and from 'having-to-become' and therefore freedom from rebirth. But it is important to realise that the epithet "freedom-from" can be misleading. For it gives the idea that freedom is always from some contingent conditionality of human life. Ands so it generates a negatively sound concept of freedom. But the spiritual freedom is an absolute good. It exists in its own right eternally in God. As such, it signifies a positive notion. When attained by individuals, it signifies a condition of being one with God as in the concept of "Brahma-Nirvana" introduced in the Gita. As we have seen, the enlightened individual sees himself like a wave in the ocean. Inalienably, being one with God, he is God, but without his own individual ego-centred identity. So spiritual freedom is a "freedom-in-God". It is the timeless state of God in which there is no distinction between the experiences and the experiencer – for in the ultimate reality there is only 'experiencing' manifest as eternal creativity. 'Freedom-from' is a consequence of 'freedom-in or with' God per se. We have seen how enlightenment knocks off the bondages of attachments and puts one into the condition of freedom. Freedom presupposes the entire journey of the individual through enquiry into the whole fabric of life. One cannot begin at the 'top'. One must begin from the familiar mundane life, through understanding the nature of the self and the nature of bondage, encountering the truth in enlightenment, before one can receive the blessing of freedom.

In particular, one must comprehend the nature of 'dependency'. In ordinary life we grow up to be dependent on others. Starting from parents, family and friends, we grow up to be dependent on social institutions and politics. Look at how small and nervous one feels with an uncertain national identity. We forget that social and cultural identities are there as functional necessities. They are not natural parts of our being. But because of our dependencies we get attached to them and therefore cannot relate to people as true human beings. We begin to recognise others, in the first place, through the labels we attach to them – black and white, Indian and non-Indian, Hindu and Christian, etc. But "dependence" is a psychological relation and a major condition of our bondage. In a spiritual quest of the self, we have to begin understanding our bondage at this level of human relationships. Our escalation into spirituality is connected with our freedom at the ground level of day-to-day existence.

The other area of our dependency, much pronounced in the modern culture of consumerism, is the area of 'gadgets' and technological innovations generally which are put to commercial use. These are believed to make our lives more comfortable and enable us for a faster and faster pace of life. Today the pace of life is so fast that we have no time to wait a moment, to look back, to consolidate and asses the real worth of our achievement. In fact, we no longer hold those values which can serve as the criteria of true worth of our lives and achievements as human beings. All 'values' have been collected and usurped by the value of money. All achievements, even in the arts and social works, are assessed in terms of status which is gained through money or power translated into money. A true social worker who works only for the intrinsic worth of his work is hard to find. So our dependency to money is super strong.

Dependency stalls a crude, callous and manipulative 'attitude' of mind. It spills around self-centred emotions which are typical of "attachment". One is uncaring, easily driven to cruelty and lives one's life largely for domination rather than for love and compassion. These two are completely different kind of lives. The whole structure of emotions surrounding the life of love is different from those surrounding the life of domination, epitomised by money. Love is liberating, money is enslaving, it is the same with the whole spectrum of articles flooding our markets today, which are supposed to make our life easier. All the consumerist culture is enslaving because soon we forget the functional value of the articles used and begin to depend upon for their luxury and status value.

So again, understanding life has to begin at this level of our relationship with things. We have to learn to situate them where they belong and for what they are worth and liberate ourselves from their domination in living. Unless we liberate ourselves at this level we will go on being driven by unccnscious impulses, round and round, in the same web of attractions, confusions and illusions, until one day your life is snatched away from you into the same darkness you came from. For most of us the whole life never sees a moment of great beauty, a moment of sudden, motionless enthralment which liberates consciousness from the entanglements of the past and brings it back into the undivided unity of 'all life'.

On the other hand, on the ethical side too, various forms of wickedness generate dependencies. First, it is well known how various forms of addiction which weaken the will discourage one to engage in doing morally good things. And psychological addition to the evil and ugly is the greatest source of dependencies. All morally evil acts and wicked temptations produce weakness of the will and character and land you into the condition of bondage to the world. It is not often realised how damaging moral wickedness is to a sane and creative human existence. The propensity to repeat a successful wicked act is the strongest in human behaviour. Moral wickedness is that kind of addiction which transforms a human being into a week and ugly animal. By contrast, the strength and the beauty of a morally good character does not create the condition of bondage. There is no such thing as addiction to morally good behaviour. This is so because goodness is rooted in love and compassion, while wickedness is rooted in selfish desire for power, wealth and pleasure. All acts producing weakness and ugliness in life are bound to produce dependencies through addiction, and cause bondage. On the other hand, goodness is liberating and free from the start. Of course, there are some people who are obsessively 'virtuous'. But self-conscious and obsessive virtuosity is almost always selfish disguise. It is selfish in the sense that the obsessive man is acting in order to promote his self-image under the label "virtuous". He has eyes always on some further gain from promoting that image.

So freedom from dependencies can be experienced right here in a day-to-day relationship. When you are free from a certain object, person or situation, your relationship with that thing is completely changed. You go through the experiencing of that object etc. without a sense of possessing or retaining that in your memory as "my experience". Experiencing" is a living thing, it is a "going through", moment to moment, being without becoming. But "experiences" are fossilised deposits of life, which one can only remember vaguely, without the vitality of a living thing. If life is extended to experiencing only, without 'storage' as a personal past, then there is no bondage to life. But there is no experience of freedom as such. Rather, in experiencing freedom from dependencies, one is experiencing the same life in a different mode of consciousness, which can be described as "non-accumulative mode". It is a mode in which consciousness has regained its creative vitality by being moment to moment new, without becoming, fossilised in experiences. Freedom is the moment to moment creativity of consciousness without being captured by thought. It is the eternity of "experiencing" without becoming somebody's "experiences". Love is the essence of this mode of consciousness when life is lived without being "possessed".

8

Epilogue

The network of self-knowledge, together with the knowledge of its source in the human condition, serves as the springboard for escalation into the moment of enlightenment. Self-knowledge by itself does not constitute enlightenment. We have explored the geography of self-knowledge. We have seen how our day-to-day behaviour springs from our personality. And we have seen how our motivational structure is eventually anchored to the primeval fear and insecurity which itself is a function of the fear of non-being. It is not possible to eliminate this fear empirically through mental action alone, since whatever we may do by way of mediation or control of will or emotion, will always be, secretly, itself a manifestation of the said fear. The fear of non-being, as we have said, is the result of our perception of the nature of consciousness by means of thought i.e. conceptually. We see that the principal and foundational element in our existence – the being of consciousness – is itself broken up into temporal mental states and events and there is no security that it will last in me for ever. This perception is bound to generate fear and consequently a life of becoming and attachment as sketched above.

The empirical, psychological, self-knowledge of this form has no spiritual significance. It can help the individual strengthen his personality traits, so that he can seek security more efficiently. For example, one who finds a certain talent in him may exploit it fully to receive financial and emotional security through it. And this, all in all, the basic pattern of life remains the same. It doesn't change anything since it doesn't eliminate your fundamental illusions and fear. That is something which is deemed to be a result of enlightenment, that is freedom, Moksha or Nirvana, signifying one's entry into the abode of the eternal.

As we have noted above, the desire to continue psychologically is one main feature of human existence. And it realises itself by setting up a permanent mode of being through "becoming". Subsequently this becoming, psychologically, determines the whole movement of life.

But in this perspective man is caught up in a paradoxical situation. The embodied existence of man has created the belief that each of us is a completely separate individual entity. He is a self which remains the same throughout his life. But when he looks upon himself psychologically he neither perceives this entity nor perceives its continuity in terms of consciousness. Consciousness, as we have said, is perpetually disturbed and conscious life has a broken existence. So one has to redefine oneself continually. Inwardly this amounts to giving oneself new psychological identities. One does that by identifying oneself as the subject or the 'owner' of all one's perceptions, which are continuously changing. This is the process of becoming. But this is paradoxical. In order to be he has to keep becoming, implying that he can never truly be.

From the beginning of thought, perhaps man has always thought in terms of becoming, which, in the light of his belief that he is a separate, permanent, individual entity, is inherently unsatisfactory. Shankara in his philosophy of non-dualism has resolved this paradox as follows: Consider a wave in the ocean, the wave wants to become the ocean by becoming big and mighty but it can't. After a while it wilts into nothing. Obviously, the wave believes that it is a separate individual entity. It is focused on its identity only as a wave. But the wave is not separate from the ocean in a "detachable" sense of the word. The wave is an undetachable part of the ocean and in that sense the wave is the ocean. If only the wave realises this, its focus will shift from its limited identity as a wave and it will see itself as the ocean.

In Shankara's view, the case of a human being is similar. He is under a great "illusion" of his identity as a separate individual and forgetful of the fact that he is really and inseparably identical with the vastness of being or Brahman. In the phenomenal world, he appears to be detachable from being at death and go into annihilation. But this is simply an illusion. The vastness of life, of which he is an undetachable part, has no beginning and no end. Self-knowledge brings this truth home. When the individual has understood the whole process of self-construction through attachments and perceived his emergence as the subject of conscious states pinned in a temporal string, then his illusion is lifted. This is the moment of enlightenment. He acquires a new perspective upon life and truth.

The practical effect of the lifting of the said illusion is that he halts the process of becoming. There is no need to want to become psychologically, anything, as you are already everything. This, however, does not mean that the individual stops living his life as an individual on the earth. But the central motivation for living as 'becoming' drops out. One lives now for the love of life.

Thought is an exercise of a concept. A concept represents a limited knowledge of a so-and-so, from the point of view of experience. Therefore a complete knowledge of the self cannot be entirely based in thought.

Particular forms of life can exist only within a 'system'. Individual human beings live within the system we call a society. But a society can exist only in constant interaction with the larger 'whole' we call 'nature'. Within the system every particular is interconnected and value-interdependent. If something goes wrong in one part of its then it must he repaired or else the whole machine will shut down.

The characteristic features of a system:

1. The health of the whole is important for the health of an item within and vice versa. There is a lesson for human being here: "Think of the well being of the whole not of yourself only".
2. A symtem serves a purpose, take a 'house', if entrance is build on the first floor, or no windows, etc. – no light or air. The house must breathe or else people living in it will not survive. Lesson: Any collective action should serve the whole or at least not be contrary to it.
3. Most important: A system cannot exist without "harmony" and balance within it. Violence is ruled out.

If particular forms of life can't exist except within a 'system', then the complete knowledge of a particular will require knowledge of the 'whole' to which it belongs. Self-knowledge in case of human beings, therefore, can't be limited to the knowledge of their material being, that is their bodies endowed with mental attributes. Self-knowledge, as the knowledge of their existential essence will involve, therefore, the understanding of the nature and the structure of not only their bodies and minds but also of their place and their relationship with the whole system of which they are a part. An individual human being who is seeking self-knowledge will naturally land himself into transcending his individual self. This is the idea behind 'knowing the essence' of the self. A complete self-knowledge, therefore, will refer you, eventually, to the knowledge of the whole truth and in that sense to the knowledge of the ultimate being or Brahman.

To seek fulfilment of desire is the great folly.

1. Desire: The peculiarity of desire-satisfaction is this. You are never completely satisfied in the sense of finality. In suitable circumstances you will desire it again. There is never a time when you will say: I am fully satisfied and don't want that satisfaction again. Further, if by chance you do say this, there is immediately another desire similar to the previous one and you want that to be satisfied. And the important thing is that there is no end to similar things to be desired for their satisfaction. So there is never a sense of completion. Something is always left over.
2. The second reason for giving up desire completely – is the nature of spiritual reality itself. Reality is complete there is nothing lacking in it. If you are in touch with it you have an extraordinary sense of completeness, beauty, vitality and fulfilment. Nothing remains to be desired.

   To enter that state: you can enter that state only when you have stopped, given up desiring altogether including the desiring of that state itself and that is possible only when you have seen the truth of the above two propositions deeply, not only verbally but experientially. Faith in the above truths is essential, which will come if to begin with you have seen it intellectually, emotionally and devotionally. But seeing the stupidity of desire-satisfaction deeply may be sufficient.

3. Moreover, desire is a form of seeking to 'become' psychologically. Human reality is defined by the desire to be – to see oneself like this or that, to become under this or that title as rich or famous or powerful etc. But all becoming is an illusion because it is relational – it exists only in a particular society, in a particular genre. In one's being, ontologically, one doesn't become anything different from what one is. And what one is, is in the hands of reality, independently of your will. So seeking to become through desire fulfilment is chasing an illusion.

In the stiritual context the world is seen as a bondage to the human spirit. This world is constructed as a network of personal attachments. At the centre of this world lies the empirical self or the ego – the "I" or the "me-consciousness". In this world there is the greatest illusion of permanence, both of the world and of the self. We see that everything is coming into being and passing away. But we do not like this state of affairs, this fact of constant creation and dissolution we wish to hold on to our personal past and to the things which belong to us. We wish to bestow upon both, the self and the world, an appearance of permanence and delude ourselves into believing it to be true. It is this service that the bonds of attachment provide. They give us a sense of "being thereness" of what is really no longer there.

In this world of attachments we create a real past and contemplate a real future to come. But the contemplated future is only psychological since, obviously, it is not yet here and now to be real. And by a similar token, the past is surely not real, or else it would not be dead and buried in the soil of memories. And furthermore there is the all important question of how real could possibly be the personal past and the personal future, when the person, as we have seen, himself is not real. We have to remember that the 'person' in question here is the empirical self or the individual ego, and not the universal person.

Again, the objects in this world of attachments are psychological, created by memories alone. I believe in my personal identity as delivered by memory. Who or what I am is a matter of remembering past experiences of certain acts and events, and certain relationships. Similarly, memories of objects of pleasure create bonds of attachment. It is the whole network of attachments which constitutes 'my' world in which I operate. My ambition and aspirations arise in this world. My actions are geared to fulfilment in this world. The whole significance of life is assessed in terms of success of my attachments. And the real goal of liberation or moksha has no chance of fulfilment in the activities of this world. From the spiritual point of view then this world is unreal and wholly insignificant.

True Worship

Religion is all about love of God and not about fear of the Lord or prayer or flattery of the Lord to get some reward in after life. Actions based on fear are always covertly selfish. Love cannot be defined in words, but one can understand it 'operationally'. When you really love someone you show immense care and goodwill towards the loved one. You can never think of hurting the person or causing any form of harm to that person. You have an enlightened attitude towards her needs and wishes, and a respect for her self-expression. It is the same thing when you love your pet animal or your garden or your music or whatever. To live for the love of life is not to be ambitious or an 'achiever' of your own self—centred desires. Rather, it is to open up to the world and enter into a creative relationship with it, enhancing its beauty and vitality in all aspects of its existence. So, obviously, to love God in real life is to enter in that form of relationship with His entire creation in which He is manifest. In the Gita, Krishna speaking as the incarnate God says:

> Earth, Water, Fire, Air,
> Space, Mind, Intelligence and
> the 'I' are all different manifestations
> of my own eightfold nature.

Even for those worshippers who do not believe in incarnation, love of God could only mean loving His entire creation.

But man is destroying the earth, hurting all its living creatures and distorting natural evolutionary processes. Violence and selfishness have become the very foundation of contemporary societies. A truly religious man, therefore, should rebel against this way of living. Through love of God, relating himself in extreme care and compassion, to all the 'manifestations of God's nature', the religious man should realise that God is accessible for worship only through His manifestation in all His "eightfold nature". We worship Him truly only in loving Him, and we love Him truly only in living our lives for the love of life in which He is manifest. In love, the religious person has put aside his personal 'hidden agenda' of ambition and acquisition of wealth and fame etc. in favour of 'doing one's best" creatively, in whatever he has undertaken to do. His attitude is to let the rewards of his action come to him naturally without aiming at them. He is unlamenting and cares little if they do not come and feels humbled and inspired if they do come.

Index